Collins need to know?

Woodworking

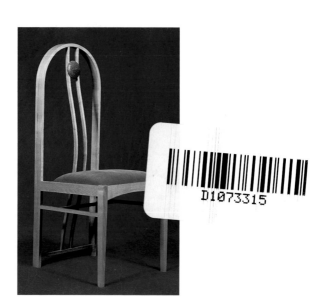

Collins need to know?

Woodworking

All the kit, techniques and inspiration
you need to work with wood

Albert Jackson & David Day

First published in 2005 by Collins
an imprint of HarperCollins*Publishers*
77–85 Fulham Palace Road
Hammersmith, London W6 8JB

www.collins.co.uk

Collins is a registered trademark of HarperCollins Publishers Limited.

09 08 07 06 05
6 5 4 3 2 1

ISBN 0 00 720573 2
© HarperCollins*Publishers*, 2005

Created by: **Focus Publishing**, Sevenoaks, Kent
Editor: Guy Croton
Designer: Neil Adams
Cover design: Sarah Christie
Front cover photograph: Todd Pearson/Getty Images

Text: Albert Jackson and David Day
Illustrators: Robin Harris and David Day
Studio Photography: Neil Waving and Ben Jennings

Designer/makers: Bill Brooker (examples of joints); Julian Rendall, p1; Nick Neenan, p6; David Pye,
p8; John Hunnex, p23 top; Derek Pearce, p24 top left; Stewart Linford, p24, top right; Mike Scott,
p24 bottom left; Raymond Winkler, p166; Derek St Romain, p177; Richard Williams, p178 bottom

*The publishers would also like to thank the following companies and individuals for kindly supplying
photographs*: Buckinghamshire Chilterns University College, pp1, 6, 166, 178 bottom; Council of
Forest Industries Canada, West Byfleet, Surrey, p26; Cuprinol Ltd, pp3 right, 172; Gavin Jordan, p18;
International Festival of the Sea (Peter Chesworth), p23 bottom; Karl Danzer, Maldon, Essex pp2 left,
20; Langlows Products Division – Palace Chemicals Ltd, Chesham, Bucks, p181; Malaysian Timber
Company, p40; Robert Bosch Ltd, p160; Ronseal Ltd, p178; Simo Hannelius, pp14, 68; Stewart
Linford Furniture, High Wycombe, Bucks, p177; Wagner Europe, p2 right

Colour reproduction by Colourscan, Singapore
Printed and bound by Printing Express Ltd, Hong Kong

contents

introduction

For centuries craftsmen have worked with wood, one of the most versatile and widely available of all building materials. Nowadays, anyone can try their hand at this most rewarding of pastimes, but a basic understanding of certain woodworking principles and techniques is crucial to success.

Introduction to woodworking

Woodworking encompasses turning, woodcarving, marquetry, cabinetmaking and joinery, but every specialist craftsman or craftswoman has at some time mastered the fundamentals of measuring and marking, assembling and finishing – the basic woodworking skills that are at the core of this book.

Woodworking is a fascinating and rewarding pastime, but it would be misleading to imply that it is easy or to suggest that a book is going to turn you into a competent craftsperson. Marking out wood for a project requires an ability to think in three dimensions, and to imagine how one component fits with another. You also need to know which tools will give the best results, and the properties of the wood you are using. Practical experience is by far the most effective teacher, and all this book can hope to do is cajole, encourage and guide you in the right direction, so you have more chance of picking up good habits rather than bad ones, and to provide you with a sound foundation upon which you can build.

▼ Cut and carved from solid cherry, rosewood and walnut, these bowls are decorated with precise fluting.

Setting up a workshop

It is hard to work without having a safe and well-organized workshop. You could convert a spare room into a small workshop, but only if you plan to use the minimum of handtools. Where possible, make use of an outbuilding, such as a garage. Being quite large, there will be easy access for raw materials, and light and power is probably already installed.

▲ Even non-electric handtools will produce dust when working with wood, so locate your workshop where dust, fumes and noise will not be a nuisance.

MUST KNOW

Health and safety in the workshop
It is advisable to protect yourself from harmful dust, fumes and, when using power tools, from flying particles and noise.

- **Safety spectacles** Made from tough impact-resistant polycarbonate plastic and designed with side screens to protect eyes from dust and wood particles.
- **Goggles** The rigid lenses of safety goggles are surrounded with a soft plastic frame that fits and seals against the contours of your face. The sides are ventilated to prevent condensation.
- **Face mask** A simple face mask stops you inhaling fine dust. Paper and gauze masks are available, and some have replaceable filters.
- **Respirator** A professional dual-cartridge respirator provides full protection against the harmful effects of toxic dust and fumes.
- **Hearing protectors** Earplugs and padded ear muffs, or ear defenders as they are often called, protect your hearing from over exposure to noise. Always wear protectors when using noisy power tools that could cause long-term damage.

▲ Safety spectacles

▲ Goggles

▲ Face mask

▲ Respirator

▲ Hearing protectors

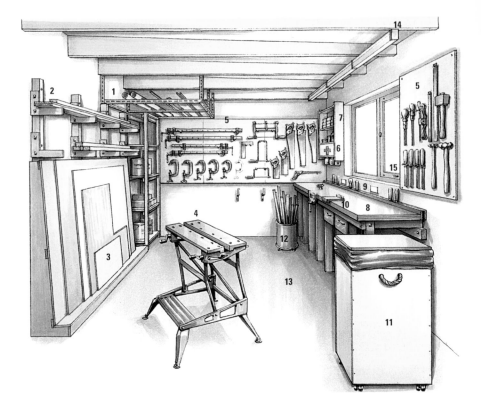

Equipping a workshop

The workshop shown above is designed for a small garage or large garden shed. If the width of your workspace does not allow a large fitted bench along one side, as shown on the right of the drawing, construct one against the shorter end wall or use a freestanding cabinetmaker's bench. Even if you don't have an extensive range of tools at the moment, allow ample storage space and plan for additional tools and equipment that you may acquire in the future.

▲ **Inside a well-equipped workshop**

1 Long-term storage *Wooden mouldings, etc., suspended on a metal-angle rack*
2 Storing wood
3 Storing man-made boards
4 Folding bench *Useful for gripping and supporting workpieces of all shapes and sizes, a folding bench can be used for jobs around the house as well as in the workshop*
5 Tool racks
6 First-aid kit *Place a well-stocked first-aid kit in an accessible and conspicuous position*
7 Small items
8 Workbench
9 Electrical sockets
10 Bench storage
11 Waste bin
12 Scrap box
13 Assembly area
14 Lighting
15 Security *Fit secure locks to windows and doors to deter burglars and children*

Workbenches

There are numerous commercially made woodworking benches, available in various lengths and widths, but having a standard height of 810mm (2ft 8in); most manufacturers also supply made-to-order benches of any height. The cabinetmaker's bench has the most useful features, including two vices and some form of tool storage.

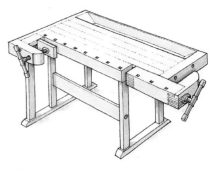
▲ Scandinavian-style bench

Cabinetmaker's benches

Most benches are constructed entirely from hardwood, although less costly softwoods are sometimes used for the underframe. Underframes are usually constructed from two mortise-and-tenoned endframes joined together with stretcher rails that are securely bolted to the legs, making transportation of the bench easier.

Worktops
Most worktops are made from a tough, close-grain hardwood, such as beech or maple, though some are partly constructed from plywood. A composite construction is perfectly acceptable, provided that the top is thick enough.

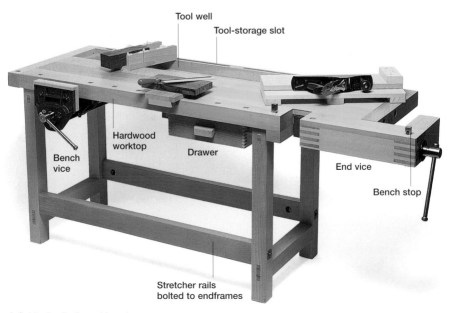

Tool well

Tool-storage slot

Hardwood worktop

Bench vice

Drawer

End vice

Bench stop

Stretcher rails bolted to endframes

▲ Cabinetmaker's workbench

Folding bench

If you have no workshop, or space is limited, you can buy a portable bench that folds flat for storage.

The worktop comprises two wide boards that form the vice jaws, one of which can be adjusted by turning a cranked handle at each end. Holes drilled in both halves of the worktop accommodate plastic clamping pegs which act as bench stops for gripping awkwardly shaped workpieces on the bench.

▲ Folding bench

▲ Continental-style vice

Woodworking vices

Continental-style vices are made with thick wooden jaws to grip the work. Another type of vice has cast iron jaws lined with wood to protect pieces from bruising. Both designs are operated by turning a tommy-bar handle on the front jaw. Some metal vices are also equipped with a quick-release lever that disengages part of the screw mechanism, allowing the jaw to be opened and closed rapidly by a straight pull or push.

An end vice provides a clamping force along the bench to hold a workpiece between metal stops dropped into holes cut into the vice and at regular intervals along one or both edges of the worktop.

Holdfast

A holdfast is a removable bench-mounted clamp, used to hold a workpiece on the bench top. It has a long shaft that fits into a hole drilled into the top and lined with a metal collar; turning a screw presses a pivoted arm down onto the work. A second collar fitted into the leg enables you to use a holdfast to support the end of a long board held in the bench vice.

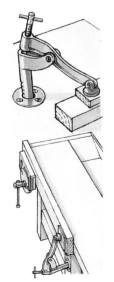
▲ Using a holdfast

Workshop storage

In the past, woodworkers usually kept their tools in sturdy chests, but it is more convenient to use space-saving tool racks and open shelving that you can make yourself.

Floor-standing shelving

A floor-standing shelf unit is the most useful form of general storage space. Make the uprights from 50 x 50mm (2 x 2in) planed softwood, joined by 50 x 25mm (2 x 1in) softwood rails bolted across the front and back. Make the shelves from 18mm (3⁄4in) man-made board, not more than 750mm (2ft 6in) wide and 300mm (1ft) deep. Screw stiff metal strips diagonally across the back to brace the frame.

▲ Floor-standing shelving

▲ Wall-mounted shelving

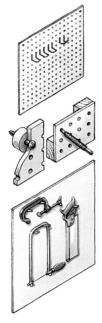

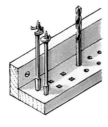

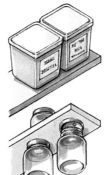

▲ Wire-hook and pegged tool racks

▲ Storing drill bits and other small items

want to know more?

Take it to the next level...

Go to...
▶ **Supporting the work** – page 88
▶ **Protecting yourself from dust** – page 161

Other sources
▶ **Evening classes**
    investigate your local adult education programme for woodworking or carpentry lessons
▶ **Internet**
    visit The Toolpost at www.toolpost.co.uk for advice on products, books and videos for the woodworking beginner
▶ **Books and Magazines**
    Practical Woodworking magazine

directory

# of wood

There are many different kinds of wood, with numerous individual properties and characteristics that lend themselves to different purposes and methods of woodworking. Wood basically falls into two distinct categories – softwood and hardwood – both of which we examine in detail in this chapter.

▶ # The origins of wood

Trees, whether growing in forests or standing alone, not only help control our climate but also provide habitats for a vast number of plants and living creatures. Tree derivatives range from natural foodstuffs through to extracts used in manufacturing products such as rubber and pharmaceuticals. When cut down and converted into wood, trees provide an infinitely adaptable and universally useful material.

▲ Gymnosperms – needle-leaved trees

▲ Angiosperms – broadleaved trees

What makes a tree? Botanically, trees belong to the Spermatophyta – a division of seed-bearing plants which is sub-divided into Gymnospermae and Angiospermae. The former are needle-leaved coniferous trees, known as softwoods, and the latter are broadleaved trees that may be deciduous or evergreen; these are known as hardwoods. All trees are perennials, which means they continue their growth for at least three years.

The main stem of a typical tree is known as a bole or trunk, and carries a crown of leaf-bearing branches. A root system both anchors the tree in the ground and absorbs water and minerals to sustain it. The outer layer of the trunk acts as a conduit to carry sap from the roots to the leaves.

Nutrients and photosynthesis

Trees take in carbon dioxide from the air through pores in the leaves called stomata, and evaporation from the leaves draws the sap through minute cells (see overleaf). When the green pigment present in leaves absorbs energy from sunlight, organic compounds are made from carbon dioxide and water. This reaction, called photosynthesis, produces the nutrients on which a tree lives, and at the same

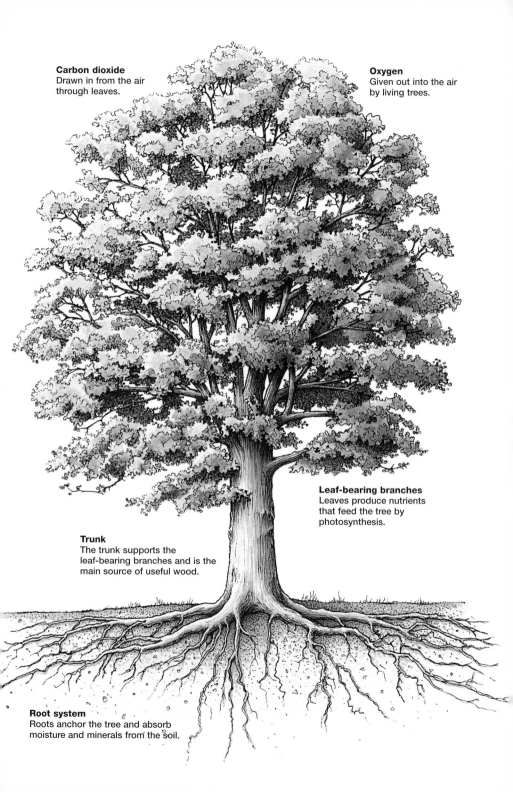

Carbon dioxide
Drawn in from the air
through leaves.

Oxygen
Given out into the air
by living trees.

Leaf-bearing branches
Leaves produce nutrients
that feed the tree by
photosynthesis.

Trunk
The trunk supports the
leaf-bearing branches and is the
main source of useful wood.

Root system
Roots anchor the tree and absorb
moisture and minerals from the soil.

▲ Mature montane coniferous forest

time gives off oxygen into the atmosphere. The nutrient produced by the leaves is dispersed down through the tree to the growing parts, and is also stored by particular cells.

Although it is often thought that wood 'breathes' and needs to be nourished as part of its maintenance, once a tree is felled, it dies. Any subsequent swelling or shrinking is a result of the wood reacting to its environment, absorbing and exuding moisture in a similar way to a sponge. Wood finishes, such as waxes and oils, enhance and protect the surface of wood, and to some extent help stabilize movement, but they do not 'feed' the wood.

Cellular structure

A mass of cellulose tubular cells bond together with lignin, an organic chemical, to form the structure of wood. These cells provide support for the tree, circulation of sap and food storage. They vary in size, shape and distribution, but are generally long and thin and run longitudinally with the main axis of the tree's trunk or branches. The orientation produces characteristics relating to the direction of grain, and the varying size and distribution of cells between species produce the character of wood textures, from fine to coarse.

Identifying wood

Examination of cells enables the identification of cut wood as being a softwood or hardwood. The simple cell structure of softwoods is composed mainly of tracheid cells, which provide initial sap conduction and physical support. They form regular radiating rows and make up the main body of the tree.

Hardwoods have fewer tracheids than softwoods; instead, they have vessels or pores which conduct sap, and fibres that give support.

MUST KNOW

New wood
The new wood cells in a growing tree develop as either living cells which store food for the tree, or non-living cells which conduct sap up the tree and provide support for it.

How trees grow

A thin layer of living cells between the bark and the wood – the cambium – sub-divides every year to form new wood on the inner side, and phloem – bast – on the outside. As the inner girth of the tree increases, the old bark splits and new bark is formed by the bast. Cambial cells are weak and thin-walled; in the growing season, the bark can be easily peeled.

▼ Cross section of a European-oak trunk

Bark
The outer protective layer of dead cells. The term 'bark' can also include the living inner tissue.

Bast or phloem
The inner bark tissue that conducts synthesized food.

Cambium layer
The thin layer of living cell tissue that forms new wood and bark.

▲ European oak
Quercus petraea

Sapwood
The new wood, the cells of which conduct or store nutrients.

Annual-growth ring
The layer of wood formed in one growing period, made up of large earlywood and small latewood cells.

Ray cells
Radiating sheets of cells that conduct nutrients horizontally; also called 'medullary rays'.

Heartwood
The mature wood that forms the tree's spine.

Pith
The central core of the tree. This can be weak and often suffers from fungal and insect attack.

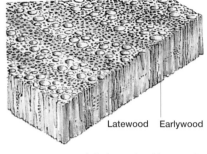

Latewood   Earlywood

▲ Earlywood and latewood

Each year, a new ring of sapwood is built up on the outside of the previous year's growth. At the same time, the oldest sapwood nearer the centre is no longer used to conduct water; it is chemically converted into the heartwood that forms the structural spine of the tree. The area of heartwood increases annually, while the sapwood remains at around the same thickness during the tree's life.

Ray cells

Ray cells, or medullary cells, radiate from the centre of the tree. They carry and store nutrients horizontally through the sapwood, in the same way as the cells that follow the axis of the trunk.

MUST KNOW

Earlywood and latewood
Earlywood is the rapid part of the annual-growth ring that is laid down in spring. Latewood grows more slowly in the summertime, with thicker cells.

Sapwood

Sapwood can usually be recognized by its lighter colour, which contrasts with the darker heartwood. However, this difference is less distinct on light-coloured woods, particularly softwoods.

Heartwood

The dead sapwood cells that form heartwood have no further part in the tree's growth, and can become blocked with organic material. Hardwoods with blocked cells – white oak, for instance – are impervious and much better suited to tasks such as barrel or cask making than woods like red oak, which have open heartwood cells and are thus relatively porous.

Annual rings

The banding made by earlywood and latewood corresponds to one season's growth and enables the age of a felled tree, and the climatic conditions through which it has grown, to be determined. Generally, wide annual rings indicate good growing conditions, narrow ones poor or drought conditions, but study of the annual rings can tell the history of the tree's growth in detail.

▲ Young hardwood forest

Properties of wood

In many woodworking projects, the grain pattern colour and texture are the most important factors when choosing which woods to work. Though equally important, the strength and working characteristics are often a secondary consideration – and when using veneer, appearance is everything.

Grain

The mass of the wood's cell structure constitutes the grain of the wood, which follows the main axis of the tree's trunk. The disposition and degree of orientation of the longitudinal cells create different types of grain.

Random and undulating grain form a variety patterns in wood, according to the angle to the surface and the way light reflects off the cell structure. Boards with these types of configurations are particularly valued for veneer.

Figure

The term 'grain' is also used to describe the appearance of wood; however, what is really being referred to is a combination of natural features collectively known as the 'figure'. These features include the difference in growth between the earlywood and latewood, the way colour is distributed, the density, concentricity or eccentricity of the annual-growth rings, the effect of disease or damage and how the wood is converted.

Using figure

When tree trunks are tangentially cut, the plain-sawn boards display a U-shape pattern. When the trunk is radially cut or quarter-sawn, the series of parallel lines usually produces a less distinctive pattern.

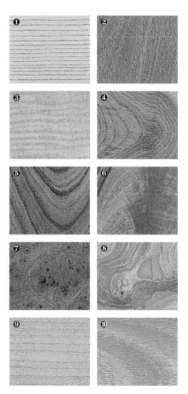

▲ **Textures and patterns**
❶ Straight grain (sitka spruce)
❷ Wavy grain (fiddleback sycamore)
❸ U-shape pattern (blackwood)
❹ Burr wood (elm)
❺ Fine-textured (lime)
❻ Spiral grain (satinwood)
❼ Wild grain (yellow birch)
❽ Curl or crotch (walnut)
❾ Stumpwood (ash)
❿ Coarse-textured (sweet chestnut)

WORKING WOOD

Planing 'with the grain' follows the direction of the grain where the fibres are parallel or slope up and away from the direction of the cutting action, resulting in smooth, trouble-free cuts. Planing a surface 'against the grain' refers to cuts made where the fibres slope up and towards the direction of the planing action; this produces a rough cut.

▲ Planing with the grain

▲ Planing against the grain

Texture

Texture refers to the relative size of the wood's cells. Fine-textured woods have small, closely spaced cells, while coarse-textured woods have relatively large cells. The difference in texture between earlywood and latewood is important to the woodworker, as lighterweight earlywood is easier to cut than the denser latewood. Those woods with even-textured growth rings are generally the easiest to work and finish.

The distribution of hardwood cells can have a marked effect on wood texture. The 'ringporous' hardwoods, such as oak or ash, have clearly defined rings of large vessels in the earlywood, and dense fibres and cell tissue in the latewood; this makes them more difficult to finish than the 'diffuse porous' woods, such as beech.

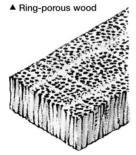
▲ Ring-porous wood

▲ Diffuse-porous wood

Durability

Durability refers to a wood's performance when it is in contact with soil. Perishable wood is rated at less than five years, and very durable at more than 25 years. The durability of a species can vary according to the level of exposure and climatic conditions.

The versatility of wood

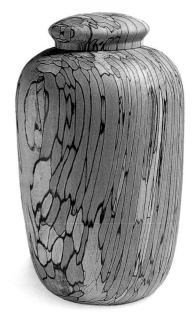

The uses to which wood can be put seem endless. So common has it become in our everyday environment that it is often taken for granted and hardly recognized for its value.

With the development of edged tools, for centuries mankind has been able to fashion wood to change and enhance the environment. Even with the development of synthetic materials and the progress of automated, mechanized production of wood, the raw material is still processed by traditional methods to meet a never-ending demand for products made from this most desirable natural material.

▲ **Lidded container**
Spalted wood, caused by fungal attack, is much prized by woodturners for its decorative patterns. Here, the black 'zone lines' and mottled colouring produce a unique random design that is exploited by the woodturner.

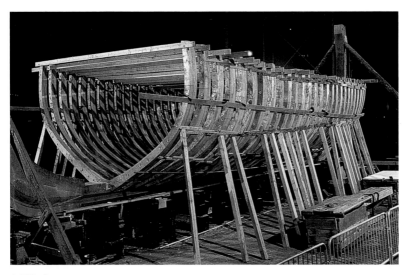

▲ **Ship frames**
Oak has long been used in traditional building construction and shipbuilding. Here, massive curved-oak frames are fitted to a keel to construct a replica of John Cabot's ship, *The Matthew*; the original crossed the Atlantic in 1497.

▲ 'Seal table'
The natural colour and texture of a 'found' piece of European sycamore log are creatively transformed into this delightful carved seal. The wood also forms the base for a clear-glass table top that represents the surface of water.

▲ Windsor chair
Typically made of turned spindles, steam-bent bows and solid, shaped seats, traditional Windsor chairs are classic examples of the chairmaker's art. They are made in various regional styles, using native woods – such as ash, elm, yew, oak, beech, birch, maple or poplar – and can be found, in original or reproduced forms, in homes around the world.

▲ Burr bowl
Solid burr wood is a favourite material for woodturners. In this striking example, the natural contours and textures of elm burr are accentuated by flaming the workpiece with a blowtorch during turning; the turned grooves and smooth inner surface add textural contrast.

▲ Shaker box
The simple design and fine craftsmanship of the American Shaker sect are clearly seen in this handmade traditional oval box. Thin-cut cherry wood is steamed and bent round a former before the projecting 'fingers' are secured by copper rivets; solid-wood ovals are then pinned into the lid and body.

The colour of wood

It is the nature of wood to be as varied in its colour as in its figure and texture. Even when prepared and finished, wood will continue to respond to its environment, changing colour or 'patina' as it ages.

Colour change

The most dramatic changes in colour occur when a finish is applied. The softwoods and hardwoods illustrated here are actual-size samples, illustrating the wood before and after the application of a clear surface finish.

Silver fir

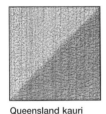
Queensland kauri

Parana pine

Cedar of Lebanon

Yellow cedar

Rimu

Larch

Norway spruce

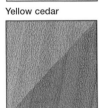
American cherry

African padauk

American white oak

Japanese oak

American red oak

Red lauan

Brazilian mahogany

Teak

Selecting wood

The selection of a suitable wood for a project is usually based on the appearance of the material and its physical and working properties.

MUST KNOW

Imperial and metric measurements
The timber trade is an international business which uses both the imperial and metric system.

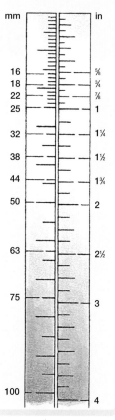

Buying wood

Timber suppliers usually stock the softwoods most commonly used for carpentry and joinery – spruce, fir and pine. They are generally sold as 'dimension' or 'dressed' stock, the trade terms for sawn or surface-planed sections cut to standard sizes. One or more of the faces may be surfaced.

Most hardwoods are sold as boards of random width and length, although some species can be bought as dimension stock.

Grading woods

Softwoods are graded for evenness of grain and the amount of allowable defects, such as knots. Hardwoods are graded by the area of defect-free wood: the greater the area, the higher the grade. The most suitable grades for general woodworking are 'firsts' and 'FAS' (firsts and seconds).

▲ Stacks of boards at a timber yard

Defects in wood

If wood is not dried carefully, stresses can mar it or make it difficult to work. Check the surface for obvious faults, such as splits, knots and uneven grain. Look at the end section, to identify how the wood was cut from the log, and to spot any distortion. Sight along the length to test for twisting or bowing. Look for evidence of insect attack.

❶ Surface checking
This is usually found along the rays. It is caused by too-rapid drying of the surface.

❸ Honeycomb checks
These occur when the outside of the board stabilizes before the inside is dry. The inside shrinks more than the outside, resulting in torn internal fibres.

❹ Shakes
These splits in the structure of the wood are caused by growth defects or shrinkage stresses. Cup or ring shakes are splits between the annual-growth rings.

❺ Dead or encased knots
These are the remains of dead branch stumps overgrown by new annual-growth rings. The wood surrounding a knot has irregular grain and is difficult to work.

❼ Ingrown bark
This can mar the wood's appearance and weaken its structure.

bow

twist or wind

spring

❷ End splits
Such splits are common defects, caused by exposed ends drying too rapidly. Sealing the ends of stacked boards with waterproof paint can prevent them.

❺ Bowing or warping
This is caused by badly stacked boards, wild grain or stresses caused by poor seasoning. Reaction wood is also prone to twist or 'cast' when cut or dried.

▶ # Softwoods of the world

Softwood timber comes from coniferous (cone-bearing) trees belonging to the botanical group Gymnospermae – plants that have exposed seeds. It is this scientific grouping, rather than their physical properties, that determines which trees are classed as softwoods.

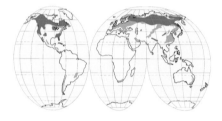

When converted into boards, softwoods can be identified by their relatively light colours, ranging from pale yellow to reddish brown. Other characteristic features are the grain pattern created by the change in colour and density of the earlywood and latewood.

■ Coniferous forest

■ Mixed forest (coniferous and deciduous broadleaved trees)

▲ **Distribution of softwoods**

Softwood-producing regions of the world

The majority of the world's commercial softwoods come from countries in the northern hemisphere. These range from the Arctic and subarctic regions of Europe and North America down to the southeastern parts of the USA.

▲ **Softwood seedling**

Cultivated softwoods

Grafting, crossbreeding and carefully controlled pollination are just some of the methods used today to produce fast-growing trees.

CONE-BEARING TREES

Although cone-bearing trees are mostly depicted as having a tall, pointed outline, this is not true of all conifers. Most are evergreens, with narrow, needle-like leaves.

Yellow cedar   Larch   Hoop pine   Parana pine

Softwoods are generally cheaper than hardwoods and are used in building construction, joinery and the manufacture of paper and fibreboard.

Botanical classification

The softwood samples on the following pages are listed alphabetically by the botanical classification of each genus and species. These are given in small type below the heading, which is the main commercial name. Other local or commercial names appear at the beginning of the text.

Colour changes

Wood is as varied in its colour as in its figure and texture. Furthermore, the colour alters over time, becoming lighter or darker. However, the most dramatic changes occur when a finish is applied – even a clear finish enriches and slightly darkens natural colours. With the description of each species, you will find a square photograph showing what the wood looks like before and after the application of a clear finish.

BUYING SOFTWOOD BOARDS

Local sawmills will sell you whole home-grown timber boards. These can come complete with bark and waney edge (the uncut edge of the board).

In contrast, imported boards are usually supplied debarked or square-edged.

Waney edge ▶

Silver fir

Abies alba

Other names: Whitewood.

Sources: Southern Europe, Central Europe.

Characteristics of the tree: A straight, thin tree, growing to about 40m (130ft) in height and 1m (3ft 3in) in diameter.

Characteristics of the wood: The pale-cream wood resembles Norway spruce (*Picea abies*), with straight grain and a fine texture. Prone to knots and is not durable.

Common uses: Building construction, joinery, plywood, boxes, poles.

Workability: It can be worked easily, using sharp handtools and machine tools to produce a very smooth finish. It glues well.

Finishing: It takes stains, paints and varnishes readily.

Average dried weight: 480kg/m³ (30lb/ft³).

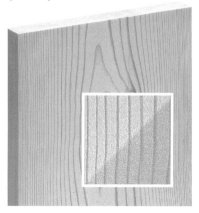

Queensland kauri

Agathis spp.

Other names: North Queensland kauri, South Queensland kauri.

Sources: Australia.

Characteristics of the tree: Although it can grow to more than 45m (150ft) high and 1.5m (5ft) in diameter, overcutting has led to a scarcity of larger trees; medium-size ones are the most common.

Characteristics of the wood: The straight-grained wood is not durable and varies in colour from pale cream-brown to pinkish brown, with a fine, even texture and lustrous surface.

Common uses: Joinery, furniture.

Workability: It can be worked readily and glues well.

Finishing: It accepts paints, stains and polishes well.

Average dried weight: 480kg/m³ (30lb/ft³).

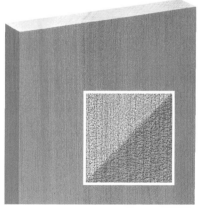

Parana pine
Araucaria angustifolia

Other names:
Brazilian pine (USA).
Sources: Brazil,
Argentina, Paraguay.
**Characteristics of
the tree:** It can reach
about 36m (120ft)
in height, with a flat crown of foliage
at its top. The trunk can be up to
1m (3ft 3in) in diameter.
Characteristics of the wood:
The mostly knot-free wood has
barely perceptible growth rings, an
even texture and straight grain. It is
not durable, and should be well-
seasoned. The core of the
heartwood is dark brown.
Common uses: Joinery, furniture,
plywood, turnery.
Workability: It is an easy wood to
work. It glues well.
Finishing: It accepts paints, stains
and polishes well.
Average dried weight: 530kg/m³
(33lb/ft³).

Hoop pine
Araucaria cunninghamii

Other names: Queensland pine.
Sources: Australia, Papua New
Guinea.
Characteristics of the tree:
This tall, elegant tree, with tufts of
foliage at the tips of thin branches,
is not a true pine. The average
height is about 30m (100ft); the
trunk diameter is about 1m (3ft 3in).
Characteristics of the wood:
The versatile wood is not durable; it
has straight grain and a fine texture.
The heartwood is yellow-brown in
colour, while the wide sapwood is
light brown.
Common uses: Building
construction, joinery, furniture,
turnery, pattern-making, plywood.
Workability: The wood can be
worked easily. It glues well.
Finishing: It accepts paints and
stains well, and can be polished to
an attractive finish.
Average dried weight: 560kg/m³
(35lb/ft³).

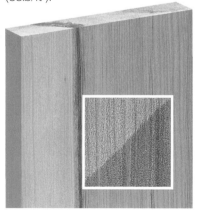

Cedar of Lebanon

Cedrus libani

Other names: True cedar.

Sources: Middle East.

Characteristics of the tree: This tree has large low-growing branches and a distinctive broad crown of foliage. Height: 40m (130ft); diameter: 1.5m (5ft).

Characteristics of the wood: The aromatic wood is soft and durable, though brittle, with straight grain. The heartwood is light brown in colour.

Common uses: Building construction, joinery, interior and exterior furniture.

Workability: Knots can be difficult to work.

Finishing: It accepts paints and stains well, and can be polished to a very fine finish.

Average dried weight: 560kg/m^3 (35lb/ft^3).

Yellow cedar

Chamaecyparis nootkatensis

Other names: Alaska yellow cedar, Pacific coast yellow cedar.

Sources: Pacific coast of North America.

Characteristics of the tree: This elegant conical-shaped tree grows slowly. Height: 30m (100ft); diameter: 1m (3ft 3in).

Characteristics of the wood: The durable pale-yellow wood has straight grain and an even texture. When dry, it is stiff, stable, relatively light and very strong.

Common uses: Furniture, veneers and high-class joinery (doors, windows, flooring, etc.), boatbuilding, oars and paddles.

Workability: It can be cut to fine tolerances and glues well.

Finishing: It accepts paints and stains well, and can be polished to a fine finish.

Average dried weight: 500kg/m^3 (31lb/ft^3).

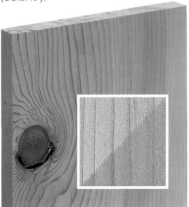

Rimu

Dacrydium cupressinum

Other names: Red pine.

Sources: New Zealand.

Characteristics of the tree: Tall and straight. Height: 36m (120ft); diameter: 2.5m (8ft).

Characteristics of the wood: The moderately durable wood has straight grain and a fine even texture, with pale-yellow sapwood that darkens to a reddish-brown heartwood.

Common uses: Interior furniture, decorative veneer, turnery, panelling, plywood.

Workability: It can be worked well with handtools and machine tools. It can be planed to a fine texture and brought to a smooth finish. It glues well.

Finishing: It can be stained satisfactorily, and finished well with paints or polishes.

Average dried weight: 530kg/m³ (33lb/ft³).

Larch

Larix decidua

Other names: None.

Sources: Europe, particularly mountainous areas.

Characteristics of the tree: One of the toughest softwoods, larch sheds its needles in winter. Height: 45m (150ft); diameter: 1m (3ft 3in).

Characteristics of the wood: The resinous wood is straight-grained and uniformly textured; it is relatively durable in outside use. The sapwood is narrow and light-coloured, and the heartwood is orange-red.

Common uses: Boat planking, pit props, joinery, posts and fencing.

Workability: The wood can be worked relatively easily with handtools and machine tools; it sands well.

Finishing: It can be painted and varnished satisfactorily.

Average dried weight: 590kg/m³ (37lb/ft³).

Norway spruce

Picea abies

Other names: European
whitewood, European
spruce, whitewood.
Sources: Europe.
**Characteristics
of the tree**: This is
an important timber-
producing tree. Height: up to 60m
(200ft); diameter: 2m (6ft 6in).
Characteristics of the wood:
The non-durable, lustrous wood is
straight-grained and even-textured,
with almost-white sapwood and pale
yellow-brown heartwood.
Common uses: Interior building
construction, flooring, boxes,
plywood.
Workability: It can be worked easily
with handtools and machine tools,
and cuts cleanly. It glues well.
Finishing: It accepts stains well, and
can be finished satisfactorily with
paints and varnishes.
Average dried weight: 450kg/m³
(28lb/ft³).

Sitka spruce

Picea sitchensis

Other names: Silver
spruce.
Sources: Canada,
USA, UK.
**Characteristics
of the tree**: This is a
widely cultivated tree.
Height: 87m (290ft); diameter:
5m (16ft).
Characteristics of the wood:
The non-durable wood is usually
straight-grained and even-textured,
with cream-white sapwood and
slightly pink heartwood.
Common uses: Building
construction, interior joinery, aircraft
and gliders, boatbuilding, musical
instruments, plywood.
Workability: It can be worked easily
with handtools and machine tools.
It glues well.
Finishing: It stains, paints and
varnishes well.
Average dried weight: 450kg/m³
(28lb/ft³).

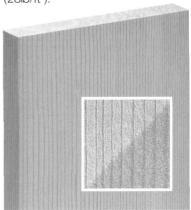

Sugar pine
Pinus lambertiana

Other names:
Californian sugar pine.
Sources: USA.
Characteristics of the tree: It typically reaches about 45m (150ft) in height and 1m (3ft 3in) in diameter.
Characteristics of the wood: The even-grained wood is moderately soft, with a medium texture. It is not durable. The sapwood is white, and the heartwood a pale-brown to reddish-brown colour.
Common uses: Light building construction, joinery.
Workability: It can be worked well with handtools and machine tools. It glues well.
Finishing: It can be brought to a satisfactory finish with stains, paints, varnishes and polishes.
Average dried weight: 420kg/m³ (26lb/ft³).

Western white pine
Pinus monticola

Other names: Idaho white pine.
Sources: USA, Canada.
Characteristics of the tree: Height: 37m (125ft); diameter 1m (3ft 3in).
Characteristics of the wood: The wood has straight grain and an even texture, with fine resin-duct lines. It is not durable. Both earlywood and latewood are pale yellow to reddish brown in colour. In many respects it is similar to yellow pine (*Pinus strobus*), but it is tougher and shrinks slightly more.
Common uses: Building construction, joinery, boatbuilding, built-in furniture, pattern-making.
Workability: It is easily worked with handtools and machine tools. It glues well.
Finishing: It accepts paints and varnishes well, and can be polished to a good finish.
Average dried weight: 450kg/m³ (28lb/ft³).

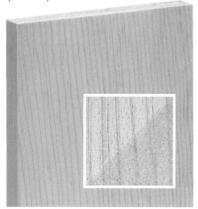

Ponderosa pine

Pinus ponderosa

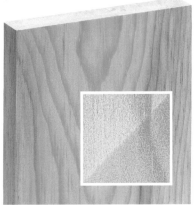

Other names:
British Columbian
soft pine (Canada);
Western yellow pine,
Californian white
pine (USA).
Sources: USA, Canada.
Characteristics of the tree:
Height: 70m (230ft); diameter:
750mm (2ft 6in).
Characteristics of the wood:
The non-durable wood can be
knotty.
Common uses: Sapwood for
pattern-making, doors, furniture,
turnery. Heartwood for joinery and
building construction.
Workability: Knots can cause
problems when planing. It glues
well.
Finishing: It takes paints and
varnishes satisfactorily.
Average dried weight: 480kg/m³
(30lb/ft³).

Yellow pine

Pinus strobus

Other names:
Quebec pine,
Weymouth pine (UK);
Eastern white pine,
Northern white pine
(USA).
Sources: USA, Canada.
Characteristics of the tree:
Height: 30m (100ft); diameter: 1m
(3ft 3in).
Characteristics of the wood:
Although the wood is soft, weak and
not durable, it is stable. It has straight
grain and a fine even texture.
Common uses: High-class joinery,
light building construction, furniture,
engineering, pattern-making, carving.
Workability: It can be worked easily
with handtools and machine tools,
providing they are kept sharp. It
glues well.
Finishing: It accepts stains, paints
and varnishes, and polishes well.
Average dried weight: 420kg/m³
(26lb/ft³).

European redwood

Pinus sylvestris

Other names: Scots pine, Scandinavian redwood, Russian redwood.

Sources: Europe, Northern Asia.

Characteristics of the tree: Height: 30m (100ft); diameter: 1m (3ft 3in).

Characteristics of the wood: Although the resinous wood is stable and strong, it is not durable unless treated.

Common uses: Building construction, interior joinery, turnery, plywood. Selected knot-free timber is used for furniture.

Workability: The wood works well with handtools and machine tools. It glues well.

Finishing: It stains satisfactorily and accepts paints and varnishes well.

Average dried weight: 510kg/m³ (32lb/ft³).

Douglas fir

Pseudotsuga menziesii

Other names: British Columbian pine, Oregon pine.

Sources: Canada, Western USA, UK.

Characteristics of the tree: Height: up to 90m (300ft); diameter: 2m (6ft 6in).

Characteristics of the wood: The straight-grained reddish-brown wood is moderately durable.

Common uses: Joinery, plywood, building construction.

Workability: It works well with handtools and machine tools that have sharp cutting edges, and glues satisfactorily. It can be finished smooth, but latewood may be left proud of the surface after sanding.

Finishing: Latewood can be resistant to stains; earlywood takes them relatively well. Both accept paints and varnishes satisfactorily.

Average dried weight: 510kg/m³ (32lb/ft³).

Sequoia

Sequoia sempervirens

Other names:
Californian redwood.
Sources: USA.
Characteristics of the tree: Height: 100m (300ft); diameter: 4.5m (15ft).
Characteristics of the wood: Despite being relatively soft, the straight-grained reddish-brown wood is durable and suitable for exterior use. The texture can vary from fine and even to quite coarse, and there is a marked contrast between earlywood and latewood.
Common uses: Exterior cladding, interior joinery, coffins, fence posts.
Workability: So long as cutting edges are kept sharp to prevent break-out along the cut, it can be worked well with handtools and machine tools. It glues well.
Finishing: It sands and accepts paints and polishes well.
Average dried weight: 420kg/m³ (26lb/ft³).

Yew

Taxus baccata

Other names:
Common yew,
European yew.
Sources:
Europe, Asia Minor, North Africa, Myanmar, Himalayas.
Characteristics of the tree: Height: 15m (50ft); diameter: 6.1m (20ft).
Characteristics of the wood: The wood is hard and durable, with a decorative growth pattern.
Common uses: Furniture, carving, interior joinery, veneer. It is particularly good for turning.
Workability: Straight-grained wood can be machined and hand-worked to a smooth finish, but irregular-grained wood can tear and be difficult to work.
Finishing: It accepts stains satisfactorily, and can be polished to an excellent finish.
Average dried weight: 670kg/m³ (42lb/ft³).

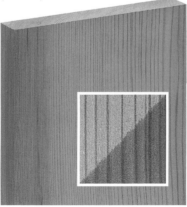

Western red cedar

Thuja plicata

Other names: Giant arbor vitae (USA); red cedar (Canada); British Columbian red cedar (UK).

Sources: USA, Canada, UK, New Zealand.

Characteristics of the tree: Height: up to 75m (250ft); diameter: up to 2.5m (8ft).

Characteristics of the wood: Although relatively soft and brittle, the non-resinous aromatic wood is durable.

Common uses: Shingles, exterior boarding, construction, furniture, cladding and decking, panelling.

Workability: It is easily worked with handtools and machine tools, and glues well.

Finishing: It accepts paints and varnishes well.

Average dried weight: 370kg/m³ (23lb/ft³).

Western hemlock

Tsuga heterophylla

Other names: Pacific hemlock, British Columbian hemlock.

Sources: USA, Canada, UK.

Characteristics of the tree: This tall, straight, elegant tree with a distinctive drooping top can reach 60m (200ft) in height and 2m (6ft 6in) in diameter.

Characteristics of the wood: The even-textured straight-grained wood is not durable and must be treated before exterior use. Pale brown and semi-lustrous, it is knot-free and non-resinous, with relatively distinctive growth rings.

Common uses: Joinery, plywood, building construction (where it is often used in place of Douglas fir).

Workability: It can be worked easily with handtools and machine tools. It glues well.

Finishing: Accepts stains, paints, polishes and varnishes well.

Average dried weight: 500kg/m³ (31lb/ft³).

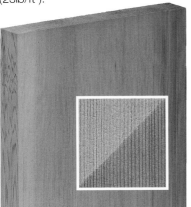

▶ # Hardwoods of the world

Hardwood trees belong to the botanical group Angiospermae – flowering broadleaved plants. Although it is this scientific grouping that determines which trees are classed as hardwoods, it is true that most hardwoods are harder than softwood timbers.

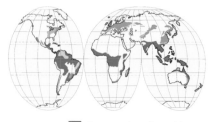

Most broadleaved trees grown in temperate zones are deciduous, losing their leaves in winter; some, however, have developed into evergreens. Broadleaved trees grown in tropical forests are mainly evergreen.

■ Evergreen broadleaved forest

☐ Deciduous broadleaved forest

☐ Mixed broadleaved forest (evergreen and deciduous)

■ Mixed forest (coniferous and deciduous broadleaved trees)

▲ **Distribution of hardwoods**

Hardwood-producing regions of the world

Climate is the primary factor in determining where species grow. For the most part, deciduous broadleaved trees grow in the temperate northern hemisphere whereas broadleaved evergreens are found in the southern hemisphere and tropical regions.

Of the thousands of species of hardwood trees found throughout the world, only a few hundred are harvested commercially. Because hardwoods are generally more durable than softwoods, with a wider range of colour, texture and figure, they are sought after and expensive.

MUST KNOW

Endangered species

Overproduction and a lack of international regulatory cooperation have led to a severe shortage of many tropical hardwoods. In the following pages, those species marked with a felled-tree symbol (as shown below) are most at risk.

▲ Planting a young hardwood tree in a tropical forest

European sycamore

Acer pseudo-platanus

Other names: Plane (Scotland); sycamore plane, great maple (UK).

Sources: Europe, Western Asia.

Characteristics of the tree: Height: 30m (100ft); diameter: 1.5m (5ft).

Characteristics of the wood: The lustrous white to yellowish-white wood is not durable and is unsuitable for exterior use, but it is good for steam-bending. It has a fine even texture.

Common uses: Turnery, furniture, flooring, veneer, kitchen utensils.

Workability: It can be worked well with handtools and machine tools. It glues well.

Finishing: It stains well, and polishes to a fine finish.

Average dried weight: 630kg/m³ (39lb/ft³).

Soft maple

Acer rubrum

Other names: Red maple (USA, Canada).

Sources: USA, Canada.

Characteristics of the tree: This medium-size tree can reach 23m (75ft) in height and 750mm (2ft 6in) in diameter.

Characteristics of the wood: The light creamy-brown wood is straight-grained, with a lustrous surface and fine texture. It is not durable and not as strong as hard maple (*Acer saccharum*), but it is good for steam-bending.

Common uses: Furniture and interior joinery, musical instruments, flooring, turnery, plywood, veneer.

Workability: The wood works readily with handtools and machine tools, and can be glued satisfactorily.

Finishing: It accepts stains well, and can be polished to a fine finish.

Average dried weight: 630kg/m³ (39lb/ft³).

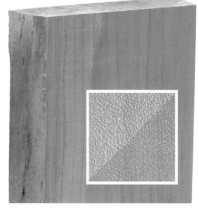

Hard maple
Acer saccharum

Other names: Rock maple, sugar maple.

Sources: Canada, USA.

Characteristics of the tree: Height: 27m (90ft); diameter of 750mm (2ft 6in).

Characteristics of the wood: The heavy wood is hard-wearing but not durable, with straight grain and fine texture. The heartwood is a light reddish brown, while the light sapwood is white.

Common uses: Furniture, turnery, musical instruments, flooring, veneer, butcher's blocks.

Workability: The wood is difficult to work with handtools or machine tools, particularly if it is irregularly grained. It glues well.

Finishing: It accepts stains, and can be polished satisfactorily.

Average dried weight: 740kg/m³ (46lb/ft³).

Western red alder
Alnus rubra

Other names: Oregon alder.

Sources: Pacific coast of North America.

Characteristics of the tree: Height: 15m (50ft); diameter: 500mm (1ft to 1ft 8in).

Characteristics of the wood: The straight-grained even-textured wood is soft and not particularly strong. It is not durable, but can be treated with preservative.

Common uses: Furniture, turnery, carving, decorative veneer, plywood, toy-making.

Workability: It can be worked well with handtools and machine tools, if cutting edges are kept sharp. It glues well.

Finishing: It accepts stains well, and can be painted or polished to a fine finish.

Average dried weight: 530kg/m³ (33lb/ft³).

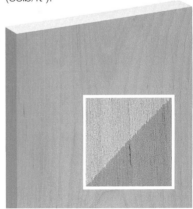

Gonçalo alves

Astronium fraxinifolium

Other names: Zebrawood (UK); tigerwood (USA).

Sources: Brazil.

Characteristics of the tree: Height: 30m (100ft); diameter: 1m (3ft 3in).

Characteristics of the wood: The medium-textured wood is hard and very durable, with hard and soft layers of material; its reddish-brown colour is streaked with dark brown and is similar to rosewood.

Common uses: Fine furniture, decorative woodware, turnery, veneer.

Workability: It is a difficult wood to work by hand. It has a natural lustre and glues well.

Finishing: It can be polished to a fine finish.

Average dried weight: 950kg/m³ (59lb/ft³).

Yellow birch

Betula alleghaniensis

Other names: Hard birch, betula wood (Canada); Canadian yellow birch, Quebec birch, American birch (UK).

Sources: Canada, USA.

Characteristics of the tree: Height: 20m (65ft); diameter: 750mm (2ft 6in).

Characteristics of the wood: The non-durable wood is usually straight-grained. It has a fine even texture and is good for steam-bending. This wood is resistant to treatment with preservatives.

Common uses: Joinery, flooring, furniture, turnery, high-grade decorative plywood.

Workability: It can be worked reasonably well with handtools, and well with machine tools. It also glues well.

Finishing: It accepts stains well, and can be polished to a fine finish.

Average dried weight: 710kg/m³ (44lb/ft³).

Paper birch

Betula papyrifera

Other names:
American birch
(UK); white birch
(Canada).

Sources: USA, Canada.

Characteristics of the tree:
Height: 18m (60ft); diameter:
300mm (1ft).

Characteristics of the wood:
The wood is fairly hard, has straight grain and a fine even texture, and is moderately good for steam-bending. It is not durable. This wood is relatively resistant to treatment with preservatives.

Common uses: Turnery, domestic woodware and utensils, crates, plywood, veneer.

Workability: It can be worked reasonably well with handtools and machine tools. It glues well.

Finishing: It accepts stains well, and can be polished to a fine finish.

Average dried weight: 640kg/m³ (40lb/ft³).

Boxwood

Buxus sempervirens

Other names:
European, Turkish,
Iranian boxwood,
according to origin.

Sources: Southern
Europe, Western Asia, Asia Minor.

Characteristics of the tree:
Height: up to 9m (30ft); diameter:
up to 200mm (8in).

Characteristics of the wood:
The wood is hard, tough, heavy and dense, with a fine even texture and straight or irregular grain.

Common uses: Tool handles, engraving blocks, musical-instrument parts, rulers, inlay, turnery, carving.

Workability: Although it is a hard wood to work, sharp tools cut it very cleanly. It glues readily.

Finishing: It accepts stains well, and polishes to a fine finish.

Average dried weight: 930kg/m³ (58lb/ft³).

Silky oak
Cardwellia sublimis

Other names: Bull oak, Australian silky oak (UK); Northern silky oak (Australia).
Sources: Australia.
Characteristics of the tree: Height: 36m (120ft); diameter: 1.2m (4ft).
Characteristics of the wood: The coarse even-textured wood is reddish brown in colour, with straight grain and large rays. It is moderately durable for exterior use.
Common uses: Building construction, interior joinery, furniture, flooring, veneer.
Workability: It works well with handtools and machine tools. Care must be taken not to tear the ray cells when planing. It glues well.
Finishing: The wood accepts stains well and can be polished to a satisfactory finish.
Average dried weight: 550kg/m³ (34lb/ft³).

Pecan/hickory
Carya illinoensis

Other names: Sweet pecan.
Sources: USA.
Characteristics of the tree: Height: 30m (100ft); diameter: 1m (3ft 3in).
Characteristics of the wood: When cut, pecan and hickory look so similar that suppliers often mix the two. The dense, tough, coarse-textured wood is similar in appearance to ash (*Fraxinus* spp.), with white sapwood and reddish-brown heartwood.
Common uses: Chairs and bentwood furniture, sports equipment, striking-tool handles, drumsticks.
Workability: If the tree has been grown fast, the dense wood will quickly dull cutting edges of handtools and machine tools.
Finishing: It can be stained and polished well, despite its porosity.
Average dried weight: 750kg/m³ (46lb/ft³).

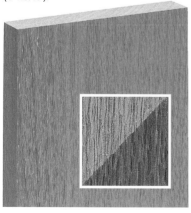

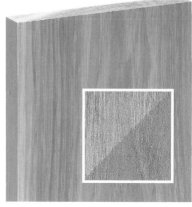

Sweet chestnut

Castanea sativa

Other names: Spanish chestnut, European chestnut.

Sources: Europe, Asia Minor.

Characteristics of the tree: Height: 30m (100ft); diameter: 1.8m (6ft).

Characteristics of the wood: The durable coarse-textured wood is yellow-brown in colour and has straight or spiral grain. The wood can corrode ferrous metals.

Common uses: Furniture, turnery, coffins, poles, stakes.

Workability: It is easy to work with handtools and machine tools, and the coarse texture can be brought to a smooth finish. It glues well.

Finishing: It accepts stains well, and can be varnished and polished to an excellent finish.

Average dried weight: 560kg/m³ (35lb/ft³).

Blackbean

Castanospermum australe

Other names: Moreton Bay bean, Moreton Bay chestnut, beantree.

Sources: Eastern Australia.

Characteristics of the tree: Height: 40m (130ft); diameter: 1m (3ft 3in).

Characteristics of the wood: The hard, heavy wood is rich brown streaked with grey-brown. Generally straight-grained.

Common uses: Furniture, turnery, joinery, carving, decorative veneers.

Workability: Softer patches of this hard wood can crumble if cutting edges are not kept sharp, so it is not particularly easy to work with handtools or machine tools. In general, it glues reasonably well.

Finishing: It accepts stains well, and can be polished to a fine finish.

Average dried weight: 720kg/m³ (45lb/ft³).

Satinwood

Chloroxylon
swietenia

Other names:
East Indian
satinwood.

Sources: Central
and Southern India, Sri Lanka.

Characteristics of the tree:
Height: 15m (50ft); diameter:
300mm (1ft).

Characteristics of the wood:
The lustrous, durable wood is light
yellow to golden brown in colour,
with a fine even texture and
interlocked grain. It is heavy, hard
and strong.

Common uses: Interior joinery,
furniture, veneer, inlay, turnery.

Workability: It is a moderately
difficult wood to work with handtools
or machine tools, and to glue.

Finishing: If care is taken, it can be
brought to a smooth surface and
polished to a fine finish.

Average dried weight: 990kg/m³
(61lb/ft³).

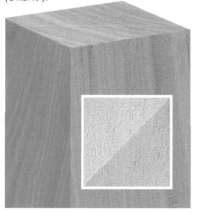

Kingwood

Dalbergia cearensis

Other names: Violet wood,
violetta (USA); bois violet
(France); violete (Brazil).

Sources: South America.

Characteristics of the tree:
This small tree, botanically related to
rosewood, produces short logs or
billets of wood up to 2.5m (8ft) long;
with the white sapwood removed,
the diameter of the billets is between
75 and 200mm (3 and 8in).

Characteristics of the wood:
This fine even-textured and durable
wood is usually straight-grained.
The dark, lustrous heartwood has a
variegated figure, striped violet-
brown, black and golden-yellow.

Common uses: Turnery, inlay,
marquetry.

Workability: It is an easy wood to
work. It glues satisfactorily.

Finishing: It can be burnished to a
fine finish, and polishes well.

Average dried weight: 1,200kg/m³
(75lb/ft³).

Sonokeling rosewood

Dalbergia latifolia

Other names: Indian rosewood.

Sources: Indonesia

Characteristics of the tree: Height: 24m (80ft) in height; diameter: 1.5m (5ft).

Characteristics of the wood: The durable wood, which is hard and heavy, has a moderately coarse uniform texture. The colour is a golden to purple brown, streaked with black or dark purple.

Common uses: Furniture, musical instruments, turnery, veneer.

Workability: It is moderately difficult to work using handtools, but machines well. It glues satisfactorily.

Finishing: Although the grain requires filling in order to achieve a high polish, it can be finished well with wax.

Average dried weight: 870kg/m³ (54lb/ft³).

Cocobolo

Dalbergia retusa

Other names: Granadillo (Mexico).

Sources: West coast of Central America.

Characteristics of the tree: Height: 30m (100ft); diameter: 1m (3ft 3in).

Characteristics of the wood: The durable, irregular-grained wood is hard and heavy, with a uniform medium-fine texture. The heartwood has a variegated colour, ranging from purple-red to yellow, with black markings.

Common uses: Turnery, brush backs, cutlery handles, veneer.

Workability: Although hard, it can be worked readily with handtools and machine tools.

Finishing: It can be stained and polished to a fine finish.

Average dried weight: 1,100kg/m³ (68lb/ft³).

Ebony

Diospyros ebenum

Other names:
Tendo, tuki, ebans.
Sources: Sri Lanka, India.
Characteristics of the tree: Height: 30m (100ft); diameter: 750mm (2ft 6in).
Characteristics of the wood: The hard, heavy, dense wood can have straight, irregular or wavy grain and has a fine even texture. The durable, lustrous heartwood is the familiar dark brown to black colour, whereas the sapwood is non-durable and is yellowish white.
Common uses: Turnery, musical instruments, inlay.
Workability: Other than on a lathe, it is a difficult wood to work. It does not glue well.
Finishing: It can be polished to an excellent finish.
Average dried weight: 1,190kg/m³ (74lb/ft³).

Jelutong

Dyera costulata

Other names: Jelutong bukit, jelutong paya (Sarawak).
Sources: Southeast Asia.
Characteristics of the tree: Height: 60m (200ft); diameter: 2.5m (8ft).
Characteristics of the wood: The soft straight-grained wood has a lustrous fine even texture and a plainish figure; it is not durable. There are usually latex ducts. Both the sapwood and heartwood are a creamy pale-brown colour.
Common uses: Interior joinery, pattern-making, matches, plywood.
Workability: It can be worked easily and brought to a smooth finish with handtools and machine tools, and is easy to carve. It also glues well.
Finishing: It accepts stains and varnishes well, and can be polished to a fine finish.
Average dried weight: 470kg/m³ (29lb/ft³).

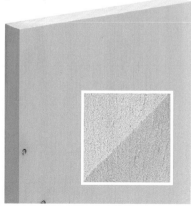

Queensland walnut

Endiandra palmerstonii

Other names:
Australian walnut, walnut
bean, oriental wood.
Sources: Australia.
Characteristics of the tree:
Height: 42m (140ft); diameter: 1.5m
(5ft).
Characteristics of the wood:
Although the non-durable wood
looks similar to that of the European
walnut (*Juglans regia*), it is not a
true walnut. The colour can vary
from light to dark brown, streaked
with pink and dark grey; the
interlocked wavy grain produces
an attractive figure.
Common uses: Furniture, interior
joinery, shop fittings, flooring,
decorative veneer.
Workability: It is a difficult wood to
work by hand or with machine tools.
Finishing: It polishes to a fine finish.
Average dried weight: 690kg/m³
(43lb/ft³).

Utile

Etandrophragma utile

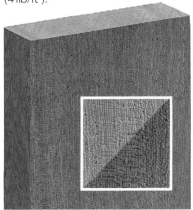

Other names:
Sipo (Ivory Coast);
assié (Cameroon).
Sources: Africa.
Characteristics of the tree:
Height: 45m (150ft); diameter: 2m
(6ft 6in).
Characteristics of the wood:
This moderately strong, durable
wood with a medium texture is
pinkish brown when freshly cut,
deepening with exposure to reddish
brown.
Common uses: Interior and
exterior joinery, boatbuilding,
furniture, flooring, plywood, veneer.
Workability: If care is taken not to
tear the ribbon-stripe figure when
planing, the wood can be worked
well. It glues satisfactorily.
Finishing: It accepts stains and
polishes well.
Average dried weight: 660kg/m³
(41lb/ft³).

Jarrah

Eucalyptus marginata

Other names: None.

Sources: Western Australia.

Characteristics of the tree: Height: 45m (150ft); diameter: 1.5m (5ft).

Characteristics of the wood: The very durable wood is strong, hard and heavy, with an even medium-coarse texture. The grain is usually straight, but can be wavy or interlocking.

Common uses: Building and marine construction, exterior and interior joinery, furniture, turnery, decorative veneers.

Workability: Although moderately difficult to work, with either handtools or machine tools, it is good for turning. It glues well.

Finishing: It polishes very well, particularly with an oil finish.

Average dried weight: 820kg/m³ (51lb/ft³).

American beech

Fagus grandifolia

Other names: None.

Sources: Canada, USA.

Characteristics of the tree: Height: 15m (50ft); diameter: 500mm (1ft 8in).

Characteristics of the wood: Slightly coarser and heavier than European beech (*Fagus sylvatica*), the straight-grained wood has similar strength and good steam-bending properties. It is light brown to reddish brown in colour, with a fine even texture.

Common uses: Cabinet-making, interior joinery, turnery, bentwood furniture.

Workability: It can be worked well with handtools and machine tools, though it has a propensity to scorch on crosscutting and drilling. It glues well.

Finishing: It accepts stains well, and can be polished to a fine finish.

Average dried weight: 740kg/m³ (46lb/ft³).

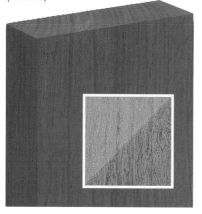

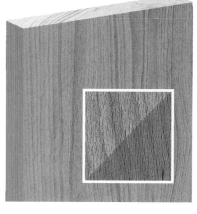

European beech

Fagus sylvatica

Other names:
English, French,
Danish beech etc.,
according to origin.

Sources: Europe.

Characteristics of the tree:
Height: 45m (150ft); diameter: 1.2m
(4ft).

Characteristics of the wood:
Whitish brown when first cut, the
fine even-textured straight-grained
wood deepens to yellowish brown
on exposure. It is a strong wood.

Common uses: Interior joinery,
cabinet-making, turnery, bentwood
furniture, plywood, veneer.

Workability: It works readily with
handtools and machine tools, but
ease of working depends on the
quality and seasoning. It glues well.

Finishing: It accepts stains well, and
can be polished to a fine finish.

Average dried weight: 720kg/m³
(45lb/ft³).

American white ash

Fraxinus americana

Other names:
Canadian ash (UK);
white ash (USA).

Sources: Canada, USA.

Characteristics of the tree:
Height: 18m (60ft); diameter:
750mm (2ft 6in).

Characteristics of the wood:
The strong shock-resistant wood is
ring-porous, with a distinct figure. It
has coarse, generally straight grain.

Common uses: Joinery,
boatbuilding, sports equipment, tool
handles, plywood, veneer.

Workability: It works well with
handtools and machine tools, and
can be brought to a fine surface
finish. It glues well.

Finishing: It accepts stains well and
is often finished in black; it can be
polished to a fine finish.

Average dried weight: 670kg/m³
(42lb/ft³).

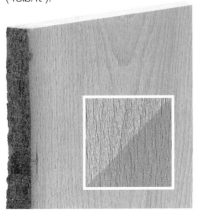

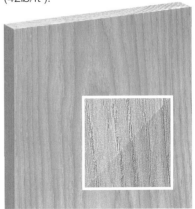

European ash

Fraxinus excelsior

Other names: English, French, Polish ash etc., according to origin.

Sources: Europe.

Characteristics of the tree: Height: 30m (100ft); diameter 500mm to 1.5m (1ft 8in to 5ft).

Characteristics of the wood: This tough coarse-textured straight-grained wood is flexible and relatively split-resistant.

Common uses: Sports equipment and tool handles, cabinet-making, bentwood furniture, boatbuilding, vehicle bodies, ladder rungs.

Workability: It can be worked well with handtools and machine tools, and can be brought to a fine surface finish. It glues well.

Finishing: It accepts stains well, and can be polished to a fine finish.

Average dried weight: 710kg/m³ (44lb/ft³).

Ramin

Gonystylus macrophyllum

Other names: Melawis (Malaysia); ramin telur (Sarawak).

Sources: Southeast Asia.

Characteristics of the tree: Height: 24m (80ft); diameter: 600mm (2ft).

Characteristics of the wood: The moderately fine even-textured wood is usually straight-grained, but sometimes the grain is slightly interlocked. Both sapwood and heartwood are a pale cream-brown colour. The wood is perishable, and not suited to exterior use.

Common uses: Interior joinery, flooring, furniture, toy-making, turnery, carving, veneer.

Workability: It can be worked reasonably well with both handtools and machine tools. It glues well.

Finishing: It accepts stains, paints and varnishes well, and can be polished to a satisfactory finish.

Average dried weight: 670kg/m³ (41lb/ft³).

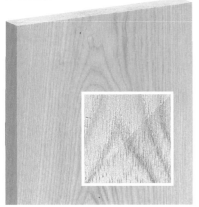

Lignum vitae

Guaiacum officinale

Other names: Ironwood (USA); bois de gaiac (France); guayacan (Spain); pala santo, guayacan negro (Cuba).

Sources: West Indies, tropical America.

Characteristics of the tree: Height: 9m (30ft); diameter: 500mm (1ft 8in).

Characteristics of the wood: This fine uniform-textured wood is one of the hardest and heaviest commercial timbers.

Common uses: Bearings and pulleys, mallets, turnery.

Workability: It is very difficult to saw and work with handtools or machine tools, but can be brought to a fine finish on a lathe.

Finishing: It can be burnished to a fine natural finish.

Average dried weight: 1,250kg/m³ (78lb/ft³).

Bubinga

Guibourtia demeusei

Other names: African rosewood; kevazingo (Gabon); essingang (Cameroon).

Sources: Cameroon, Gabon, Zaire.

Characteristics of the tree: Height: 30m (100ft); diameter: 1m (3ft 3in).

Characteristics of the wood: The hard, heavy wood has a moderately coarse even texture. Although not resilient, it is reasonably strong and durable.

Common uses: Furniture, turnery, decorative veneer (known as kevazingo when rotary cut).

Workability: Although it can be worked well with handtools and machined to a fine finish, cutting edges must be kept sharp.

Finishing: It accepts stains well, and can be polished to a fine finish.

Average dried weight: 880kg/m³ (55lb/ft³).

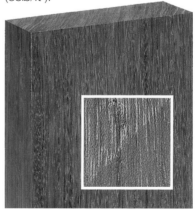

Brazilwood

Guilandina echinata

Other names:
Pernambuco
wood, bahia
wood, para wood.

Sources: Brazil.

Characteristics of the tree:
This small to medium-size tree
produces short billets or lengths up
to 200mm (8in) in diameter.

Characteristics of the wood:
The heavy, hard wood is tough,
resilient and very durable.

Common uses: Dyewood, violin
bows, exterior joinery, parquet
flooring, turnery, gun stocks, veneer.

Workability: It can be worked
reasonably well with handtools and
machine tools, as long as cutting
edges are kept sharp. It also glues
well.

Finishing: The surface can be
polished to a very fine finish.

Average dried weight:
1,280kg/m³ (80lb/ft³).

Butternut

Juglans cinerea

Other names: White walnut.

Sources: Canada, USA.

Characteristics of the tree:
Height: 15m (50ft); diameter:
750mm (2ft 6in).

Characteristics of the wood:
The coarse-textured straight-
grained wood is relatively soft and
weak, and is not durable. The figure
resembles that of black American
walnut (*Juglans nigra*), but the
medium-brown to dark-brown
heartwood is lighter in colour.

Common uses: Furniture, interior
joinery, carving, veneer, boxes,
crates.

Workability: If cutting edges are
kept sharp, it can be worked easily
with handtools and machine tools.
It glues well.

Finishing: It accepts stains well, and
can be polished to a fine finish.

Average dried weight: 450kg/m³
(28lb/ft³).

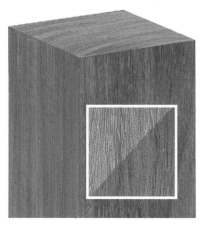

American black walnut

Juglans nigra

Other names: American walnut.
Sources: USA, Canada.
Characteristics of the tree: Height: 30m (100ft); diameter: 1.5m (5ft).
Characteristics of the wood: The tough moderately durable wood has an even but coarse texture. The grain is usually straight, but can be wavy.
Common uses: Furniture, musical instruments, interior joinery, gun stocks, turnery, carving, plywood, veneer.
Workability: It can be worked well with handtools and machine tools. It glues well.
Finishing: It can be polished to a fine finish.
Average dried weight: 660kg/m³ (41lb/ft³).

European walnut

Juglans regia

Other names: English, French, Italian walnut etc., according to origin.
Sources: Europe, Asia Minor, Southwest Asia.
Characteristics of the tree: Height: 30m (100ft). The average trunk diameter is 1m (3ft 3in).
Characteristics of the wood: The moderately durable wood has a rather coarse texture, with straight to wavy grain. It is typically grey-brown with darker streaks.
Common uses: Furniture, interior joinery, gun stocks, turnery, carving, veneer.
Workability: It can be worked well with handtools and machine tools, and glues satisfactorily.
Finishing: It can be polished to a fine finish.
Average dried weight: 670kg/m³ (42lb/ft³).

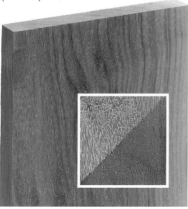

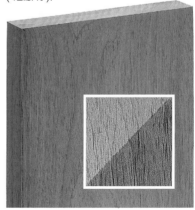

Tulipwood

Liriodendron tulipifera

Other names: Canary whitewood (UK); yellow poplar, American poplar (USA).

Sources: Eastern USA, Canada.

Characteristics of the tree: Height: 37m (125ft); diameter: 2m (6ft 6in).

Characteristics of the wood: The fine-textured straight-grained wood is quite soft and lightweight. It is not durable, and should not be used in contact with the ground.

Common uses: Light construction, interior joinery, toy-making, furniture, carving, plywood, veneer.

Workability: It can be worked easily with handtools and machine tools, and glues well.

Finishing: It accepts stains, paint and varnish well. Also polishes well.

Average dried weight: 510kg/m³ (31lb/ft³).

Balsa

Ochroma lagopus

Other names: Guano (Puerto Rico, Honduras); topa (Peru); lanero (Cuba); tami (Bolivia); polak (Belize, Nicaragua).

Sources: South America, Central America, West Indies.

Characteristics of the tree: Height: 21m (70ft); diameter: 600mm (2ft). It reaches maturity in 12 to 15 years.

Characteristics of the wood: The lustrous open-textured straight-grained wood is the lightest commercial hardwood.

Common uses: Insulation, buoyancy aids, model-making, packaging for delicate items.

Workability: If cutting edges are kept sharp to avoid crumbling or tearing, it can be worked and sanded easily. It glues well.

Finishing: It can be stained, painted and polished satisfactorily.

Average dried weight: 160kg/m³ (10lb/ft³).

Purpleheart

Peltogyne spp.

Other names: Amaranth (USA); pau roxo, amarante (Brazil); purplehart (Surinam); saka, koroboreli, sakavalli (Guyana).

Sources: Central America, South America.

Characteristics of the tree: Height: 50m (165ft); diameter: 1m (3ft 3in).

Characteristics of the wood: The wood is durable, strong and resilient. It has a uniform fine to medium texture.

Common uses: Building construction, boatbuilding, furniture, turnery, flooring, veneer.

Workability: It can be worked well, although cutting edges must be kept sharp.

Finishing: It accepts stains well and can be wax-polished.

Average dried weight: 880kg/m³ (55lb/ft³).

Afrormosia

Pericopsis elata

Other names: Assemela (Ivory Coast, France); kokrodua (Ghana, Ivory Coast); ayin, egbi (Nigeria).

Sources: West Africa.

Characteristics of the tree: Height: 45m (150ft); diameter: 1m (3ft 3in).

Characteristics of the wood: The yellow-brown heartwood of this durable wood darkens to the colour of teak (*Tectona grandis*). However, the straight to interlocked grain has a finer texture than teak.

Common uses: Veneer, interior and exterior joinery and furniture, building construction, boatbuilding.

Workability: If care is taken with interlocked grain, it saws well and can be planed smooth. It glues well.

Finishing: It can be polished to a fine finish.

Average dried weight: 710kg/m³ (44lb/ft³).

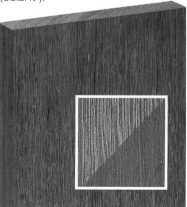

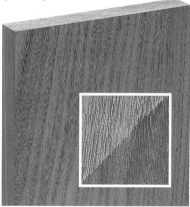

European plane

Platanus acerifolia

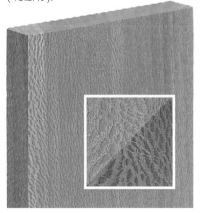

Other names: London, English, French plane etc., according to origin.

Sources: Europe.

Characteristics of the tree: Easily identified by its flaking mottled bark, this tree is often found in cities because of its tolerance of pollution. Height: 30m (100ft); diameter: 1m (3ft 3in).

Characteristics of the wood: The straight-grained fine to medium-textured wood is perishable and not suitable for exterior use.

Common uses: Joinery, furniture, turnery, veneer.

Workability: It can be worked well with handtools and machine tools.

Finishing: It accepts stains and polishes satisfactorily.

Average dried weight: 640kg/m³ (40lb/ft³).

American sycamore

Platanus occidentalis

Other names: Buttonwood (USA); American plane (UK).

Sources: USA.

Characteristics of the tree: Height: 53m (175ft); diameter: 6m (20ft).

Characteristics of the wood: The fine even-textured pale-brown wood is perishable and not suitable for exterior use. It is usually straight-grained, and distinct darker rays produce lacewood when quarter-sawn. Botanically it is a plane tree, but the wood is lighter in weight than European plane.

Common uses: Joinery, doors, furniture, panelling, veneer.

Workability: The wood works well with handtools and power tools, and glues well.

Finishing: It accepts stains and polishes satisfactorily.

Average dried weight: 560kg/m³ (35lb/ft³).

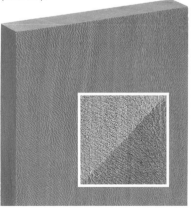

American black cherry

Prunus serotina

Other names: Cabinet cherry (Canada).

Sources: Canada, USA.

Characteristics of the tree: Height: 21m (70ft); diameter: 500mm (1ft 8in).

Characteristics of the wood: The durable wood has a straight grain and fine texture; it is hard and moderately strong, and can be steam-bent. The narrow sapwood is a pinkish colour, while the heartwood is reddish-brown to deep red, with brown flecks and some gum pockets.

Common uses: Furniture, pattern-making, joinery, turnery, musical instruments, tobacco pipes, veneers.

Workability: It can be worked well with handtools and machine tools, and glues well.

Finishing: It accepts stains well, and can be polished to a fine finish.

Average dried weight: 580kg/m³ (36lb/ft³).

African padauk

Pterocarpus soyauxii

Other names: Camwood, barwood.

Sources: West Africa.

Characteristics of the tree: Height: 30m (100ft); diameter: 1m (3ft 3in).

Characteristics of the wood: The hard, heavy wood has straight to interlocked grain and a moderately coarse texture. The pale-beige sapwood can be 200mm (8in) thick; the very durable heartwood is rich red to purple-brown, streaked with red.

Common uses: Interior joinery, furniture, flooring, turnery, handles. Also used as a dyewood.

Workability: It can be worked well with handtools, and machined to a fine finish. It glues well.

Finishing: It can be polished to a fine finish.

Average dried weight: 710kg/m³ (44lb/ft³).

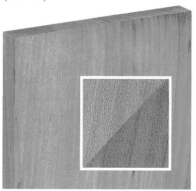

American white oak

Quercus alba

Other names: White oak (USA).

Sources: USA, Canada.

Characteristics of the tree: Height: 30m (100ft); diameter: 1m (3ft 3in).

Characteristics of the wood: The straight-grained wood is similar in appearance to European oak (*Quercus robur*), but it is more varied in colour.

Common uses: Building construction, interior joinery, furniture, flooring, plywood, veneer.

Workability: It can be readily worked with handtools and machine tools, and glues satisfactorily.

Finishing: It accepts stains well, and can be polished to a good finish.

Average dried weight: 770kg/m³ (48lb/ft³).

Japanese oak

Quercus mongolica

Other names: Ohnara.

Sources: Japan.

Characteristics of the tree: Height: 30m (100ft); diameter: 1m (3ft 3in).

Characteristics of the wood: The coarse texture of this straight-grained wood is milder than that of the European and American white oaks due to its slower, more even rate of growth. The colour is a light yellowish brown throughout. It is a good wood for steam-bending and is generally knot-free.

Common uses: Interior and exterior joinery, boatbuilding, furniture, panelling, flooring, veneer.

Workability: Compared to other white oaks, it is easy to work well with handtools and machine tools. It glues well.

Finishing: It accepts stains and can be polished very well.

Average dried weight: 670kg/m³ (41lb/ft³).

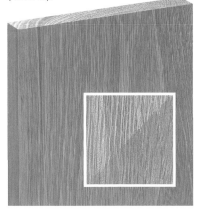

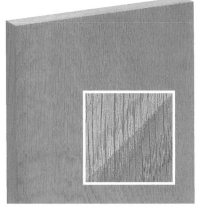

European oak

Quercus robur/
Q. petraea

Other names: French, Polish oak etc., according to origin.
Sources: Europe, Asia Minor, North Africa.
Characteristics of the tree: Height: 30m (100ft); diameter: 2m (6ft 6in).
Characteristics of the wood: The coarse-textured wood has a straight grain and distinct growth rings.
Common uses: Joinery and external woodwork, furniture, flooring, boatbuilding, carving, veneer.
Workability: It can be worked readily with handtools and machine tools. It glues well.
Finishing: Liming, staining and fuming are all possible, and it can be polished to a good finish.
Average dried weight: 720kg/m³ (45lb/ft³).

American red oak

Quercus rubra

Other names: Northern red oak.
Sources: Canada, USA.
Characteristics of the tree: Height: 21m (70ft); diameter: 1m (3ft 3in).
Characteristics of the wood: The non-durable wood has a straight grain and coarse texture, though this can vary according to the rate of growth. It is good for steam-bending.
Common uses: Interior joinery and flooring, furniture, plywood, decorative veneer.
Workability: It can be worked readily with handtools and machine tools, and glues satisfactorily.
Finishing: It accepts stains well, and can be polished to a good finish.
Average dried weight: 790kg/m³ (49lb/ft³).

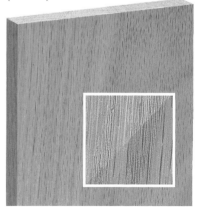

Red lauan

Shorea negrosensis

Other names: None.

Sources: Philippines.

Characteristics of the tree: Height: 50m (165ft); diameter: 2m (6ft 6in).

Characteristics of the wood: The wood is moderately durable, with interlocked grain and a relatively coarse texture. An attractive ribbon-grain figure is shown on quarter-sawn boards.

Common uses: Interior joinery, furniture, boatbuilding, veneer, boxes.

Workability: It can be worked easily with handtools and machine tools, but care must be taken not to tear the surface of the wood when planing. It glues well.

Finishing: It accepts stains well, and can be varnished and polished to a good finish.

Average dried weight: 630kg/m³ (39lb/ft³).

Brazilian mahogany

Swietenia macrophylla

Other names: Honduran, Costa Rican, Peruvian mahogany etc.

Sources: Central America, Southern America.

Characteristics of the tree: Height: 45m (150ft); diameter: 2m (6ft 6in).

Characteristics of the wood: The naturally durable wood has a medium texture, with grain that may be either straight and even or interlocked. The white-yellow sapwood contrasts with the heartwood, which is reddish brown to deep red.

Common uses: Interior panelling, joinery, boat planking, furniture, pianos, carving, decorative veneer.

Workability: It can be worked well with handtools and machine tools.

Finishing: It accepts stains very well, and can be polished to a fine finish when the grain is filled.

Average dried weight: 560kg/m³ (35lb/ft³).

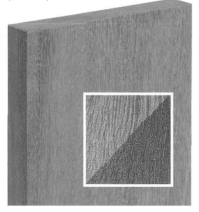

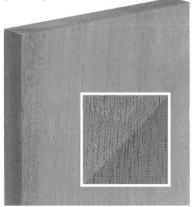

Teak

Tectona grandis

Other names: Kyun, sagwan, teku, teka.

Sources: Southern Asia, Southeast Asia, Africa, Caribbean.

Characteristics of the tree: Height: 45m (150ft); diameter: 1.5m (5ft).

Characteristics of the wood: The strong, very durable wood has a coarse uneven texture with an oily feel.

Common uses: Interior and exterior joinery, boatbuilding, turnery, exterior furniture, plywood, veneer.

Workability: It can be worked well with handtools and machine tools, but quickly dulls cutting edges. Newly prepared surfaces glue well.

Finishing: It accepts stains, varnishes and polishes, and can be finished well with oil.

Average dried weight: 640kg/m³ (40lb/ft³).

Basswood

Tilia americana

Other names: American lime.

Sources: USA, Canada.

Characteristics of the tree: Height: 20m (65ft); diameter: 600mm (2ft).

Characteristics of the wood: The straight-grained wood has a fine even texture. The soft, weak wood is cream-white when first cut, turning pale brown on exposure, with little contrast between latewood and earlywood.

Common uses: Carving, turnery, joinery, pattern-making, piano keys, drawing boards, plywood.

Workability: It can be easily and cleanly worked with handtools and machine tools, and can be brought to a fine surface finish. It glues well.

Finishing: It accepts stains well, and can be polished to a fine finish.

Average dried weight: 416kg/m³ (26lb/ft³).

Lime

Tilia vulgaris

Other names: Linden (Germany).

Sources: Europe.

Characteristics of the tree: It can reach a height of more than 30m (100ft), with a clear trunk about 1.2m (4ft) in diameter.

Characteristics of the wood: The straight-grained wood has a fine uniform texture. Although soft, it is strong and resists splitting, making it good for carving.

Common uses: Carving, turnery, toy-making, broom handles, hat blocks, harps, piano soundboards and keys.

Workability: It is an easy wood to work with handtools and machine tools, as long as cutting edges are kept sharp. It glues well.

Finishing: It accepts stains well, and can be polished to a fine finish.

Average dried weight: 560kg/m³ (35lb/ft³).

Obeche

Triplochiton scleroxylon

Other names: Ayous (Cameroon); wawa (Ghana); obechi, arere (Nigeria); samba, wawa (Ivory Coast).

Sources: West Africa.

Characteristics of the tree: Height: 45m (150ft); diameter: 1.5m (5ft).

Characteristics of the wood: The fine even-textured wood is lightweight and not durable. The grain may be straight or interlocked. There is little contrast between the sapwood and heartwood.

Common uses: Interior joinery, furniture, drawer linings, plywood, model-making.

Workability: If cutting edges are kept sharp, the soft wood is easy to work with handtools and machine tools. It glues well.

Finishes: It accepts stains, and polishes well.

Average dried weight: 390kg/m³ (24lb/ft³).

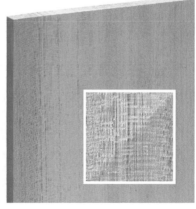

American elm
Ulmus americana

Other names: Water elm, swamp elm, soft elm (USA); orhamwood (Canada).

Sources: Canada, USA.

Characteristics of the tree: Height: 27m (90ft); diameter: 500mm (1ft 8in).

Characteristics of the wood: The coarse-textured wood is not durable. It is strong and good for steam-bending.

Common uses: Boatbuilding, agricultural implements, cooperage, furniture, veneer.

Workability: Sharp cutting edges enable it to be readily worked with handtools and machine tools. It glues satisfactorily.

Finishing: It accepts stains and polishes satisfactorily.

Average dried weight: 580kg/m³ (36lb/ft³).

Dutch and English elm
Ulmus hollandica/ U. procera

Other names: English elm: Red elm. Dutch elm: Cork bark elm.

Sources: Europe.

Characteristics of the tree: Height: 45m (150ft); diameter: up to 2.5m (8ft).

Characteristics of the wood: The coarse-textured wood has beige-brown heartwood and distinct irregular growth rings, with an attractive figure when plain-sawn.

Common uses: Cabinet-making, Windsor-chair seats and backs, boatbuilding, turnery, veneer.

Workability: Wood with irregular grain can be difficult to work.

Finishing: It accepts stains and polishes well, and is particularly suited to a wax finish.

Average dried weight: 560kg/m³ (35lb/ft³).

Plywood

Plywood is made from thin laminated sheets of wood called construction veneers, plies or laminates. These are bonded at 90 degrees to each other to form a strong, stable board; odd numbers of layers are used, to ensure that the grain runs the same way on the top and bottom.

Manufacturing plywood

A wide range of timber species of both hardwoods and softwoods is used to produce plywood. The veneers may be cut by slicing or rotary cutting – for softwoods, the latter is the most common method.

A debarked log is converted into a continuous sheet of veneer of a thickness between 1.5 and 6mm (⅙ and ¼in). The sheet is clipped to size, then sorted and dried under controlled conditions before being graded into face, or core, plies. Defective plies are plugged and narrow core plies are stitched or spot-glued together before laminating.

The prepared sheets are laid in a glued sandwich, the number depending on the type and thickness of plywood required, and hot-pressed.

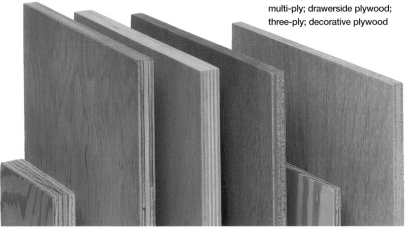

▼ Different types of plywood – left to right: six-ply; two sheets of multi-ply; drawerside plywood; three-ply; decorative plywood

DIRECTORY OF WOOD

The boards are then trimmed to size and are usually sanded to fine tolerances on both sides.

Uses of plywood

The performance of plywood is determined not only by the quality of the plies, but also by the type of adhesive used in its manufacture. Major manufacturers test their products rigorously by taking batch samples through a series of tests that exceed service requirements. The glue bond of exterior grades is stronger than the wood itself, and panels made with formaldehyde glues must comply with a formaldehyde-emissions standard.

Plywoods can be broadly grouped by usage. Types include: interior plywoods (INT), which are used for interior non-structural applications; exterior plywoods (EXT), which depending on the quality of the adhesive, can be used for fully or semi-exposed conditions; marine plywoods for boatbuilding; and structural or engineering grade plywoods for applications where strength and durability are the prime considerations.

▲ Stocks of silver birch for plywood manufacture.

APPEARANCE GRADING

Plywood producers use a coding system to grade the appearance quality of the face plies used for boards. The letters do not refer to structural performance.

Typical systems for softwood boards use the letters A, B, C, C plugged and D. The A grade is the best quality, being smooth-cut and virtually defect-free; D grade is the poorest, and has the maximum amount of permitted defects, such as knots, holes, splits and discolouration. A-A grade plywood has two good faces, unlike all others.

Grading stamps

Boards with A-grade or B-grade veneer on one side only are usually stamped on the back; those with A or B grades on both faces are usually stamped on the panel edge.

APA

A-C   GROUP 1

EXTERIOR

000
PS 1-83

▲ Stamp applied to back face.

A-B · G-1 · EXT-APA · 000 · PS1-83

▲ Stamp applied to edge.

Blockboard and laminboard

Blockboard is a form of plywood, by virtue of having a laminated construction. Where it differs from conventional plywood is in having its core constructed from strips of softwood cut approximately square in section.

This stiff material is suitable for furniture applications, particularly shelving and worktops. It makes a good substrate for veneer work, although the core strips can telegraph. It is made in similar panel sizes to plywood, with thicknesses ranging from 12mm (½in) to 25mm (1in). Boards of three-ply construction are made up to 44mm (1¾in) thick.

Laminboard

Laminboard is similar to block-board, but the core is constructed with narrow strips of softwood, each about 5mm (³⁄₁₆in) thick; these are usually glued together. Like blockboard, laminboard is made in both three- and five-ply construction. Its higher adhesive content makes laminboard denser and heavier than blockboard.

Because the core is less likely to 'telegraph' or show through, this is superior to blockboard for veneer work. It is also more expensive. Boards of three- and five-ply construction are produced. With the latter, each pair of thin outer plies may run perpendicular to the core. Alternatively, the face ply only may run in line with the core strips.

▲ Blockboard (left) and laminboard (right)

▶ Fibreboards

Fibreboards are made from wood that has been broken down to its basic fibre elements and reconstituted to make a stable homogeneous material. The density of the boards depends on the pressure applied and the type of adhesive used in the manufacturing process.

Hardboards

Hardboard is a high-density fibreboard produced from wet fibres pressed at high pressure and temperature. The natural resins in the fibres are used to bond them together.

Standard hardboard has one smooth and one textured face. It is made in a range of thicknesses, most commonly from 3 to 6mm (⅛ to ¼in), and in a wide range of panel sizes. An inexpensive material, it is often used for drawer bottoms and cabinet backs. Duo-faced hardboard is made from the same material as standard board, but has two smooth faces.

Decorative hardboard is available as perforated, moulded or lacquered boards. Perforated types are used for screens, most others for wall panelling.

▼ **Hardboards**
❶ Oil-tempered
❷ Standard
❸ Lacquered
❹ Perforated

❶   ❷   ❸   ❹

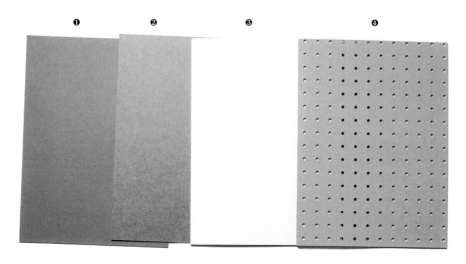

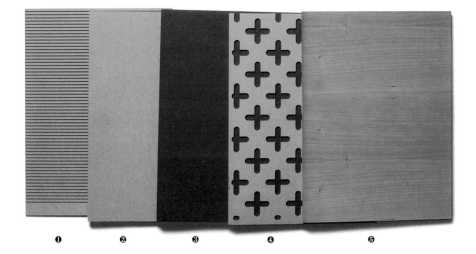

Oil-tempered hardboard is impregnated with resin and oil to produce a strong abrasion-resistant material that is also water-resistant.

Medium-density fibreboard (MDF)

Medium-density fibreboard is made by combining fine wood fibres with resins. The mix is compacted in a heated press and the end product has a smooth uniform texture. MDF can be cut, planed and moulded with ease, and the surface will take stains, paints or varnishes. Generally, thicknesses range from 3 to 30mm (⅛ to 1⅛in).

Standard MDF is ideal for interior cabinetwork, such as fitted bedroom units. Moisture-resistant boards are more suitable for the conditions found in kitchens or bathrooms. Ready-coloured MDF can be used to make children's furniture and toys. For radiator covers and screens, pierced MDF panels are sold in a range of modern and traditional designs. Specialist panel suppliers stock bendable MDF, which is grooved on one side to allow the board to be formed into curved and S-shaped components.

▲ **Medium-density fibreboards (MDF)**
❶ Bendable
❷ Standard
❸ Ready-coloured
❹ Perforated
❺ Veneered

MUST KNOW

Storing boards
To save space, man-made boards should be stored on their edges. A rack will keep the edges clear of the floor and support the boards evenly at a slight angle. To prevent a thin board bending, support it from beneath with a thicker board.

DIRECTORY OF WOOD

Particle boards

Wood-particle boards are made from small chips or flakes of wood bonded together under pressure – softwoods are generally used, although a proportion of hardwoods may be included. Various types of boards are produced.

The production of particle boards is a highly controlled automated process. The wood is converted into particles of the required size by chipping machines. After drying, the particles are sprayed with resin binders and spread to the required thickness with their grain following the same direction. This 'mat' is hot-pressed under high pressure to the required thickness, and then cured. The cooled boards are trimmed to size and sanded.

Particle boards are stable and uniformly consistent. The types of particle board most used by woodworkers are those of interior quality, which are commonly known as chipboard.

▼ **Particle boards**
❶ Single-layer chipboard
❷ Three-layer chipboard
❸ Graded-density chipboard
❹ Decorative chipboard
❺ Oriented-strand board
❻ Flakeboard or waferboard

Working man-made boards

Although man-made boards are relatively easy to cut using woodworking handtools and machines, the resin content in the boards can quickly dull cutting edges.

The boards can be awkward to handle, due to their size, weight or flexibility. Cutting a board into smaller sections requires clear space with adequate support.

Cutting by machine

Clean-cutting high-speed machine tools will give the best results when cutting man-made boards, but will dull quickly in the process. A universal saw blade with tungsten-carbide tipped teeth should be utilized for cutting a large amount of board.

Cutting by hand

A 10 to 12PPI panel saw should be used for hand-sawing; a tenon saw can be used for smaller work. In either case, the saw should be held at a relatively shallow angle. To prevent break out of the surface when severing fibres or laminate, all cutting lines should be scored with a sharp knife.

▲ Lay the board over a bench and support it close to the cut line. Cutting large boards may require a helper.

want to know more?

Take it to the next level...

Go to...
▶ **Stains and dyes** – pages 165–71
▶ **Varnishes and lacquers** – pages 172–6
▶ **Oil finishes** – page 181–3

Other sources
▶ **Associations and Clubs**
  Association of Woodturners of Great Britain (www.woodworking.co.uk). The organization has affiliated local branches throughout the country. It exists to provide education and information to those interested in woodturning
▶ **Books and Magazines**
  World Woods in Colour by William A. Lincoln (Stobart Davies)

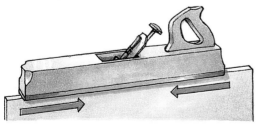

▲ Plane edges of man-made boards from both ends towards the middle, to prevent break out of the core.

tools and

techniques

Good woodworking is as much about using the right tools and techniques as it is about choosing the right wood. There is a wide selection of woodworking tools on the market today, ranging from traditional handtools that have barely changed in centuries, to high-tech machines and power tools.

Rules and tape measures

It is advisable to use the same rule or tape measure when marking out a project, in case there is any variation between one tool and another. It makes sense to buy rules and tape measures that offer both metric and imperial graduations.

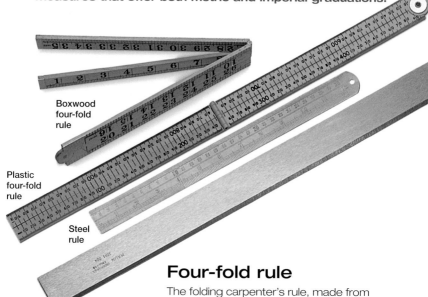

Boxwood four-fold rule

Plastic four-fold rule

Steel rule

Metal straightedge

Four-fold rule

The folding carpenter's rule, made from boxwood with brass hinges and endcaps, is still popular among traditionalists. Most folding rules are 1m (3ft) in length when fully extended. Because it is relatively thick, you have to stand a wooden rule on edge in order to transfer measurements accurately to the work. Similar rules made from plastic are sometimes made with bevelled edges to overcome this problem.

Steel rule

A 300mm (1ft) stainless-steel rule is useful for marking out small workpieces and for setting marking gauges and power-tool fences.

Straightedge

Every workshop needs at least one sturdy metal straightedge, measuring between 500mm (1ft 8in) and 2m (6ft 6in) long. A bevelled straightedge is ideal for making accurate cuts with a marking knife and for checking that a planed surface is perfectly flat. Some straightedges are etched with metric or imperial graduations.

Tape measure

Retractable steel tapes, measuring from 2 to 5m (6 to 16ft) long, are usually graduated along both edges. A lock button prevents the tape retracting automatically. Refills are usually available for replacing damaged tapes.

Some tape measures incorporate a liquid-crystal display that tells you how far the tape has been pulled from its case; a built-in memory retains the measurement when the tape is retracted.

Self-adhesive steel tapes are sold without cases for sticking along the front edge of a workbench.

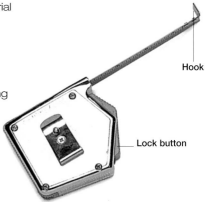

Hook

Lock button

▲ Retractable tape measure

Hook rules

To make it easier to take accurate measurements from the edge of a workpiece, use a steel rule with an integral hook at one end.

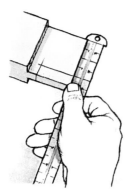

Measuring techniques

Measuring from edge to edge

When taking external measurements with a tape measure, hook the tip over one edge of the workpiece and read off the dimension against the opposite edge.

Checking for winding

If you suspect a board is twisted or 'winding', hold a steel rule across each end; if the rules appear to be parallel, the board is flat. If not, discard the board.

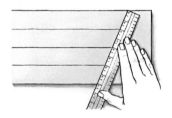

Taking internal measurements

When measuring between two components, read off the dimension where the tape enters its case, then add the length of the case to arrive at the true measurement.

Dividing a workpiece equally

You can divide a workpiece into equal parts using any rule or tape measure. Use a pencil to mark off the divisions between the lines on the rule to measure into halves, quarters, thirds, etc.

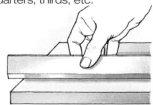

Using pinch rods

Hold two battens side by side. Draw a mark across both battens to register their relative positions – then, without releasing your grip, transfer them to the work.

Checking a surface is flat

To check that a panel is flat, place a straightedge on the surface. A bump will cause the tool to rock; chinks of light showing beneath the straightedge indicate hollows.

Squares and bevels

Squares and sliding bevels are used by woodworkers to mark out workpieces and to check the accuracy of individual components and assemblies.

Try square

The finest try squares, used to mark and check right angles, have a blued-steel metal blade riveted at 90 degrees to a rosewood stock edged with brass. A square with a 300mm (1ft) blade is best for general woodwork.

Mitre square

Used for marking-out and checking the accuracy of mitre joints, the blade of a special purpose mitre square is fixed at 45 degrees to the stock.

Sliding bevel

A sliding bevel can be employed to mark or check any angle, using the adjustable blade which is secured with a short brass lever or wing nut.

Combination squares

Although dedicated mitre and try squares are more accurate, you can buy a combination square that will serve both functions. Some try squares are made with the top inside corner of the stock cut at 45 degrees for marking out bevels, but an all-metal combination square with a sliding 300mm (1ft) blade is much more versatile. A knurled nut locks the blade in position, and most models have a spirit level built into the stock or head.

Blued-steel blade

Mitre square

Adjustable blade

Sliding bevel

Locking lever

Rosewood stock

Try square

▲ Using a combination square.

Using squares and bevels

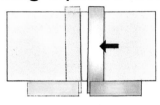

Checking a try square

Draw a line at right angles to the edge of a workpiece, turn the square over and slide the blade up to the marked line. The blade and the pencil mark will align precisely if the square is accurate.

Setting a sliding bevel

Slacken the locking lever just enough for the blade to move; set the required angle against a protractor, then retighten the lever.

Marking with a try square

Mark out square shoulders with a try square and pencil. Place the tip of the knife on the pencil line, and slide the square up to the flat side of the blade. Holding the square firmly against the face edge, draw the knife carefully along the marked line to indicate the position of cut.

Checking a mitre or bevel

Place a mitre square or sliding bevel over the bevelled face of a workpiece. Slide the tool along the bevelled face to check the angle is accurate across the workpiece.

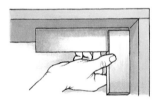

Checking a joint is square

When assembling corner joints, use a try square to check that the two components meet at a right angle.

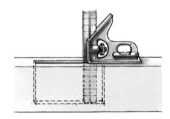

A square as a depth gauge

Slacken the knurled nut, place the tip of the blade against the bottom of the mortise and slide the head up against the edge of the work. Read the depth of the mortise.

Marking gauges

Gauges are designed to score fine fines parallel with the edges of a workpiece, usually for marking out joints or scribing rabbets (a cut made along an edge).

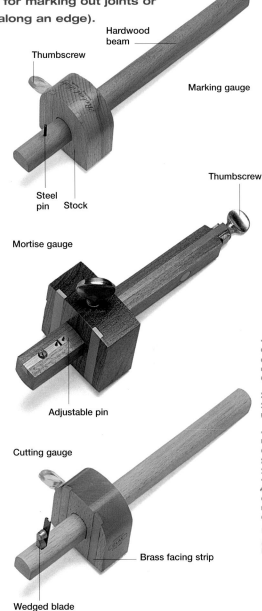

Marking gauge

A marking gauge comprises an adjustable fence or stock which slides along a hardwood beam that has a sharp steel pin driven through one end. A thumbscrew clamps the stock at any point along the beam.

Hardwood beam

Thumbscrew

Marking gauge

Steel pin

Stock

Mortise gauge

A mortise gauge is made with two pins, one fixed and the other adjustable, so that you can score both sides of a mortise simultaneously. On the best gauges the movable pin is adjustable to very fine tolerances, using a thumbscrew located at the end of the beam. Most mortise gauges have a second fixed pin on the back of the beam so that the tool doubles as a standard marking gauge.

Thumbscrew

Mortise gauge

Adjustable pin

Cutting gauge

A cutting gauge is fitted with a miniature blade instead of a pointed pin, enabling you to mark a line across the grain without tearing the wood fibres. The blade, which is held in place with a brass wedge, can be removed for sharpening. A stardard scribing blade, used for marking various corner joints, has a rounded cutting tip.

Cutting gauge

Brass facing strip

Wedged blade

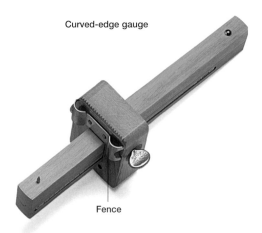

Curved-edge gauge

Fence

Curved-edge gauge

It is practically impossible to score a line parallel to a curved edge with an ordinary marking gauge. A curved-edge gauge has a brass fence that rests on two points, preventing the stock rocking as it follows the edge of the work. The same tool can also be used on straight edges, as it is a particularly versatile tool.

Panel gauge

A standard marking gauge has a 200mm (8in) beam, but there are gauges with beams up to 800mm (2ft 8in) for scribing lines on man-made boards. These panel gauges are fitted with quite wide stocks, held in place with a captive wedge or a wooden clamping screw.

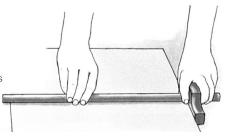

IMPROVISING A GAUGE

For carpentry that does not require absolute precision, you can gauge lines with a pencil.

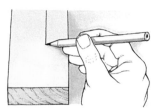

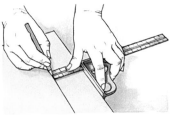

Using your fingertip
Run a fingertip against the edge of the workpiece to keep the pencil point on a parallel path. You need a steady hand to do this effectively.

Using a combination square
For slightly wider dimensions, follow the edge of the work with the head of a combination square, using the tip of the blade to guide the pencil point.

Using marking gauges

Setting a marking gauge

Some marking gauges have graduated beams that make it easy to adjust the stock, but it is usually necessary to align the pin with a rule, then slide the stock with your thumb until it comes to rest against the end of the rule.

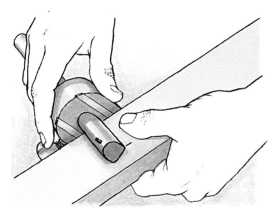

Adjusting a marking gauge

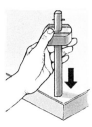

Tighten the thumbscrew and check the setting. If necessary, make fine adjustments by tapping the base of the beam against a bench to increase the distance between pin and stock. Reduce this distance by tapping the tip.

Setting a mortise gauge

Adjust the distance between the pins to match the width of a mortise chisel, then set the stock to suit the thickness of the leg or stile. Use the same pin setting to scribe a matching tenon, adjusting the stock accordingly.

Scribing with a gauge

Place the beam on the workpiece with the pin pointing towards you, then slide the stock up against the side of the work. Rotate the tool until the pin begins to mark the wood, then push the gauge away from you to scribe a clear line.

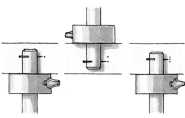

Gauging a centre line

To find the exact centre of a rail or stile, set a marking gauge as accurately as possible, then check the measurement by making a single pin prick, first from one side of the workpiece, then from the other. If the pin pricks fall short or overshoot the centre line, adjust the gauge until they coincide.

Handsaws

Handsaws are designed for converting planks of solid wood and man-made boards into smaller pieces, ready for planing. The best handsaws are skew-backed, having a gentle S-bend to the top of the blade which reduces the weight of the saw and improves its balance. The same blades are usually thinner, to provide better clearance in the kerf (cut made by a saw).

Ripsaw

The largest handsaw, with a 650mm (2ft 2in) blade, is designed specifically to cut solid timber in the direction of the grain. A ripsaw has large teeth with almost vertical leading edges, and each tooth is filed straight across to produce a chisel-like cutting tip. In common with all but the smallest saws, alternate teeth are 'set', or bent to the right or left, to cut a kerf that is wider than the thickness of the blade. This prevents the saw jamming in the wood. Ripsaws are made with 5 or 6 PPI (see page 86).

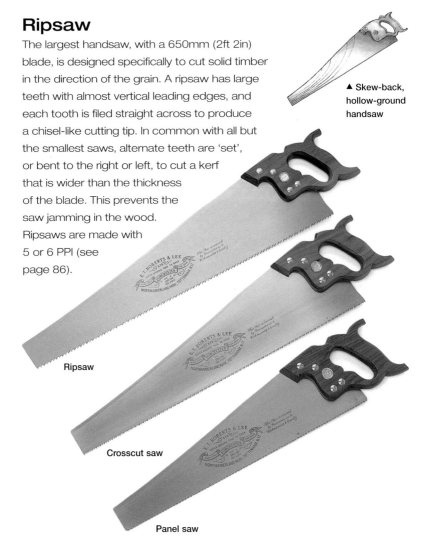

▲ Skew-back, hollow-ground handsaw

Ripsaw

Crosscut saw

Panel saw

Crosscut saw

A crosscut saw has teeth specially designed for severing solid wood across the grain, and is therefore the ideal saw for cutting planks or balks of timber to length. Each tooth leans backward at an angle or 'pitch' of 14 degrees, and is filed with a sharp cutting edge and tip that score the wood fibres on each side of the kerf. Crosscut-saw blades are between 600 and 650mm (2 to 2ft 2in) long, with 7 to 8 PPI.

Fleam-tooth saws

Fleam-tooth crosscutting saws are particularly efficient as they sever the wood on the return stroke as well as the forward. Fleam teeth have a pitch of 22.5 degrees.

Panel saw

Having relatively small crosscut teeth, at 10 PPI, a panel saw is designed primarily for cutting man-made boards to size, but doubles as a crosscut saw for severing solid wood. Panel-saw blades are between 500 and 550mm (1ft 8in to 1ft 10in) long.

Universal saw

Some manufacturers offer universal handsaws with teeth that are similar in shape to those of a crosscut saw but which cut well both with and across the grain. Universal saws are made with 6 to 10 PPI.

Frame saw

A traditional-style frame saw is designed for ripping or crosscutting solid wood, depending on which blade is fitted. The narrow blade is held under tension by a twisted-wire tourniquet that runs between the solid-wood end posts.

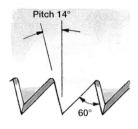

▲ Ripsaw teeth

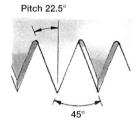

▲ Crosscut saw teeth

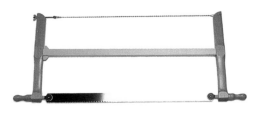

▲ Fleam-tooth saw teeth

▲ Frame saw

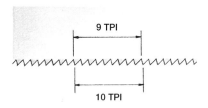

9 TPI

10 TPI

▲ Specifying saw-tooth sizes

▲ Open and closed handgrips

Saw-tooth sizes

Despite metrication, saw-tooth sizes are generally specified by the number of teeth that fit into 1in – TPI (teeth per inch) – measuring from the base of one tooth to the base of another. Alternatively, saw teeth may be specified by PPI (points per inch) counting the number of saw-tooth tips in 1in of blade. When compared, there is always one more PPI than TPI.

Saw handles

Elegant handles are still made from tough short-grain hardwood, although the majority of handsaws now have moulded plastic grips that are more economical to manufacture. The choice of material makes no difference to the performance of the saw, but make sure the handle feels comfortable to hold and check that it is set low behind the blade for maximum thrust on the forward stroke.

Open and closed grips

Some small dovetail saws and keyhole saws are made with open pistol-grip handles. However, most saws are made with stronger closed handgrips.

MUST KNOW

Caring for handsaws

Saw teeth dull quickly if saws are thrown carelessly into a tool box or if one saw blade is dragged across another. Slip a plastic guard over the toothed edge of a blade before storing it, or carry your saws in a canvas case that is made with separate pockets to house a range of saws.
  Use white spirit to clean resin deposits from a saw blade, and wipe the metal with an oily rag before you put it away.

USING A SAW AS A SQUARE

Plastic handles are sometimes moulded with shoulders set at 90 and 45 degrees to the straight back of the blade so that the saw can be used as a large try square or mitre square.

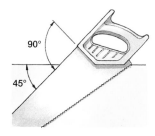

90°

45°

Using handsaws

Provided the saw is sharp and the teeth have been set properly, it is possible to work for long periods with a handsaw without tiring.

The best grip
Hold a handsaw with your forefinger extended towards the toe of the blade. This grip provides optimum control.

Starting the cut
Guiding the saw with your thumb held against the flat of the blade, make short backward strokes to establish the cut.

Following through
Saw with slow steady strokes, using the full length of the blade – with fast or erratic movements the saw is more inclined to jam or wander off line. If necessary, twist the blade slightly to bring it back on line.

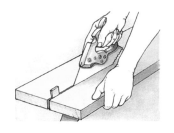

Prevent the saw jamming
If the kerf begins to close on the blade, drive a small wedge into the cut to keep it open. Otherwise, lubricate the saw by rubbing a candle on both sides of the blade.

Finishing the cut
As you approach the end of a cut, lower the saw handle slightly and make slow strokes as you sever the last few wood fibres. Support a long offcut with your free hand.

Reverse-action grip
To finish sawing a large panel, turn round and saw back towards the kerf you have just made. Alternatively, use a two-handed grip to control the saw, continuing the kerf in the same direction.

Supporting the work

You cannot hope to cut a workpiece with accuracy unless you support it properly. You can damp a piece of wood to a bench top, but you may find it more comfortable and convenient to use a pair of trestles or 'sawhorses' about 600mm (2ft) high.

Crosscutting

Bridge a pair of sawhorses with a plank of wood for crosscutting. If the workpiece is thin and whippy, support it from beneath with a thicker piece of wood.

Ripsawing

Support the work in a similar way when ripping a plank lengthways, moving each sawhorse in turn to provide a clear path for the blade. Prevent flexing by placing two planks under the board.

Crosscutting with a frame saw

When severing a plank of wood with a frame saw, cant the frame slightly to one side so that you can see the cut line clearly. Pass your free hand through the frame and behind the blade to support an offcut.

Ripping with a frame saw

Clamp the work to a sturdy bench, so that you can use two hands to control the saw, and turn the blade at 90 degrees to the frame. Grip one of the end posts with both hands, ensuring that the narrow blade cannot twist and cause the saw to wander off line.

Backsaws

Backsaws are made with relatively small crosscut teeth for trimming lengths of wood to size and for cutting woodworking joints. The special feature of all backsaws is the heavy steel or brass strip folded over the top of the blade for extra weight.

A tenon saw, having 13 to 15 PPI along a 250 to 350mm (10 to 14in) blade, is the largest and most versatile of the backsaw family.

A dovetail saw is a smaller version of the tenon saw, but the teeth are too fine – 16 to 22 PPI – to be set conventionally, relying instead on the burr produced by file-sharpening to provide the extremely narrow kerf required for cutting dovetails and similar joints.

A straight dovetail saw with a handle cranked to one side is made for trimming dowels and through tenons flush with the wood surface.

A miniature backsaw with about 26 PPI, the bead saw is ideal for cutting fine joints and model making.

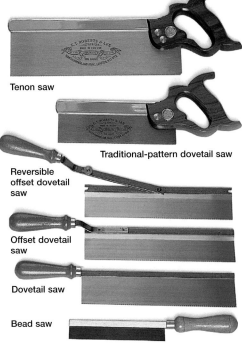

Tenon saw

Traditional-pattern dovetail saw

Reversible offset dovetail saw

Offset dovetail saw

Dovetail saw

Bead saw

Backsaw techniques

Cutting with the grain
Clamp the work in a bench vice when sawing a tenon or dovetail down to the shoulder.

Crosscutting
Holding the work securely against a bench hook (see page 119), make short backward strokes on the waste side of the line until the cut is established; then gradually lower the blade to the horizontal as you extend the kerf.

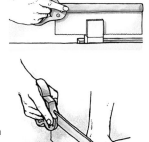

▶ Curve-cutting saws

A group of saws with narrow blades is made specifically for cutting curved shapes or holes in solid wood and boards. Various sizes and designs are available; your choice will depend on the material to be cut and the scale of the work.

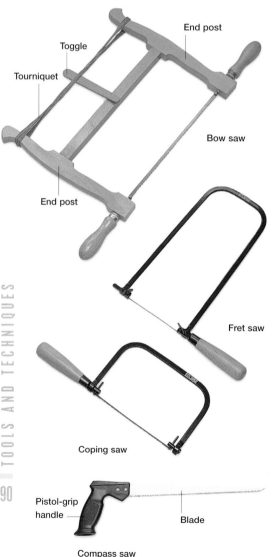

Toggle

End post

Tourniquet

Bow saw

End post

Fret saw

Coping saw

Pistol-grip handle

Blade

Compass saw

The bow saw is a medium-weight frame saw suitable for cutting relatively thick pieces of wood. It is fitted with a 200 to 300mm (8 to 12in) blade held under tension by a tourniquet that runs between the saw's end posts. The 9 to 17 PPI blades can be turned through 360 degrees to swing the frame aside

The very narrow blade of a 150mm (6in) coping saw is held under tension by the spring of its metal frame. The 15 to 17 PPI blades are too narrow to sharpen and are simply replaced when they become blunt or are broken.

Similar in construction to a coping saw, the fret saw has a deep frame that holds replaceable blades under tension. A fret saw, with its 32 PPI blades, is for cutting thin pieces of wood and board or for shaping a sandwich of marquetry veneers.

Most curve-cutting saws are limited by their frames to cutting holes relatively close to the edges of a workpiece. The frameless compass saw has a narrow, tapered blade that is stiff enough to hold its shape and thus can be used to cut a hole in a board of any thickness as far from the edges as required.

Using curve-cutting saws

Most curve-cutting saws require special techniques to counter the tendency for the weight of their frames to turn the blade off line.

Cutting with a bow saw

A bow saw requires a two-handed grip to control the direction of cut. Grip the straight handle with one hand, extending your forefinger in line with the blade. Place your free hand alongside the other, wrapping the forefinger and middle finger around the saw's end post, one on each side of the blade.

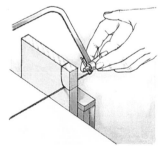

Controlling a coping saw

To prevent the blade wandering off line, place the first joint of your extended forefinger on the coping saw's frame. Then, form a double-handed grip for better control.

Using a fret saw

Thin workpieces tend to vibrate unless they are supported from below by a strip of plywood screwed to the bench top, overhanging the front edge. Cut a V-shape notch in the plywood to provide clearance for the fret saw blade.

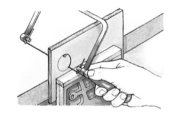

Making closed cuts

When cutting a hole with any frame saw, mark out the work and bore a small access hole for the blade, just inside the waste.

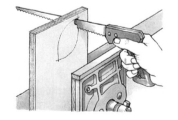

Using a compass saw

When cutting holes with a compass saw, drill a starter hole for the tip of the blade. Saw steadily to avoid buckling on the forward stroke.

Replacing blades

Curve-cutting saws are designed for quick and easy replacement of blunt, broken or bent blades.

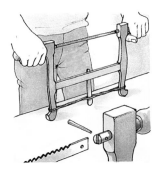

Changing a bow saw blade

Unwind the toggle to slacken the tourniquet, then locate each end of the blade in the slotted metal rods that extend from the handles. Pass the retaining pins through the rods and blade at both ends and tighten.

Fitting a fret saw blade

Fret saw blades are fitted like coping saws, but with thumbscrew clamps. With the teeth facing the handle, clamp the toe end of the blade, then flex the frame against a bench, tightening the other thumbscrew onto the blade. Releasing pressure on the frame is sufficient to put the blade under tension.

Fitting a compass saw blade

To fit a compass saw blade, slacken the screw bolts, slide the slotted end of the replacement blade into the handle and tighten.

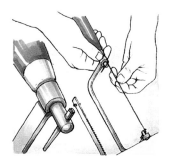

Replacing a damaged coping saw blade

Each end of a coping saw blade fits into a slotted retaining pin. To replace a damaged blade, reduce the distance between the retaining pins by turning the saw's handle anticlockwise.

Attach the blade to the toe of the saw, with the teeth facing away from the handle. Flex the frame against the edge of a bench until you can locate the other end of the blade. Tighten the handle to tension the blade; then align both pins by eye.

TOOLS AND TECHNIQUES

Hammers and mallets

Most workshops boast a range of hammers, even though they are rarely used in joint-making, except when reinforcing with pins or nails.

One medium-weight cross-peen hammer will suffice for most needs. It is heavy enough to tap joints together and dismantle them again, yet sufficiently well-balanced so that you can perform precise operations.

For very delicate work, use a lightweight cross-peen pin hammer.

You will find a claw hammer convenient for making jigs and mock-ups from softwood. Not only can you drive in large nails with ease, but you can also extract them with the split peen, using the strong shaft as a lever. Though slightly more expensive, all-metal claw hammers are even stronger than those with wooden shafts.

A carpenter's mallet is specially designed for driving chisels and gouges; its wide head is tapered so that it will strike a chisel squarely each time, and will wedge itself even more securely on the tapered shaft with each blow.

NAIL SET

A nail set is a tapered metal punch that is used with a hammer to drive nail heads below a wood surface.

Cross-peen hammer

Cross-peen hammer (square pattern)

Pin hammer

Pin hammer (square pattern)

Claw hammer

Carpenter's mallet

Chisels and gouges

Woodworking of any kind is impossible without at least a small range of well-made chisels and gouges. In jointmaking, they are especially useful for removing waste wood and for paring components to make a snug fit.

The standard woodworking chisel has a strong rectangular-section blade which you can confidently drive with a mallet through pine or hardwoods, without fear of it breaking. Firmer chisels range from 3 to 38mm (⅛ to 1½in) wide.

The slim-bladed bevel-edge chisel is designed for more delicate work, using hand pressure only. It is used primarily for shaping and trimming joints, and the bevels ground along both sides of the blade make the chisel suitable for working dovetail undercuts.

A paring chisel is a bevel-edge chisel with an extra-long blade for levelling housings. A cranked version makes it possible to pare waste from very wide joints.

The sash-mortise chisel is a specialized tool for cutting deep mortises. It is made with a tapered blade that does not jam in the work, and which is thick enough to be used as a lever when chopping waste out of a joint. The deep blade sides help keep it square to the mortise. Mortise chisels are made up to 12mm (½in) wide.

A gouge is a chisel with a blade curved in cross section. When the cutting-edge bevel is ground on the inside of the blade, it is known as an in-cannel gouge; the tip of an out-cannel blade is ground on the outside. Gouges are used to scoop waste wood out of hollows and to trim curved shoulders.

Firmer chisel

Bevel-edge chisel

Cranked paring chisel

Paring chisel

Sash-mortise chisel

In-cannel gouge

Out-cannel gouge

Planes

Bench planes are general-purpose tools used to smooth the surfaces of timber and to plane it square and true. Wooden planes are still available, but nearly all planes are now made from metal. in addition, you will need a few specialized planes for shaping and trimming joints.

Jack plane

Metal smoothing plane

Wooden smoothing plane

Jack plane

The 350mm (1ft 2in) jack plane is long enough to plane most edges accurately.

Smoothing plane

The smoothing plane is the smallest bench plane available, at 225mm (9in) long, and is ideal for final shaping and finishing of workpieces.

Block plane

A block plane (see below right) is small enough to be used single handedly, yet strong enough to take generous shavings for fast shaping and trimming. It is a good general purpose plane, much used for cutting end grain.

Rabbet plane

This is no longer an essential tool, now that power routers are widespread, but rabbeting is surprisingly fast by hand. The plane (see top page 96) has an adjustable fence and depth stop; with the

Wooden and metal block planes

Rabbet plane

Shoulder plane

Bull-nose plane

Router plane

Plough plane

Combination plane

blade mounted near the toe, you can cut stopped rabbets. The pointed spur mounted on the side of the plane scores the wood ahead of the blade when rabbeting across the grain.

Shoulder plane

A dedicated joint-cutting tool (see top), the all-metal shoulder plane is designed specifically for shaving square shoulders on larger joints.

Bull-nose plane

A miniature version of the shoulder plane, this plane (see top) is useful for trimming small joints.

Router plane

Once the preferred tool for levelling housings and hinge recesses, the hand router plane has largely been superseded by the power router.

Plough plane

An inexpensive plane, used for cutting narrow grooves parallel with an edge, this comes with a range of interchangeable cutters.

Combination plane

The sophisticated combination plane cuts even wider grooves than a plough plane, and can be used to shape a matching tongue along the edge of another component.

Dismantling and adjusting bench planes

All metal bench planes are similarly made and are dismantled in the same way. In some planes, the blade is held in place with a wedge, although most modern planes made from wood are fitted with capped blades and depth-adjustment screws.

Removing the blade and cap iron

To remove the blade for sharpening or to make other adjustments to a metal bench plane, first take off the lever cap by lifting its lever and sliding the cap backward to release it from its locking screw. Lift the blade and cap iron out of the plane, revealing the wedge-shaped casting known as the frog which incorporates the blade-depth and lateral-adjustment controls.

To separate the cap iron and blade, use a large screwdriver to loosen the locking screw, then slide the cap iron towards the cutting edge until the screw head can pass through the hole in the blade.

Cap iron locking screw
Lever cap screw
Lever
Depth-adjustment lever
Lateral-adjustment lever
Lever cap
Cap iron
Knob
Blade
Depth-adjustment nut
Frog-adjusting screw
Frog-fixing screw
Sole

▲ Components of a metal bench plane

Adjusting the frog

The cutting edge of the blade protrudes through an opening in the sole called the mouth. By adjusting the frog, you can modify the size of this

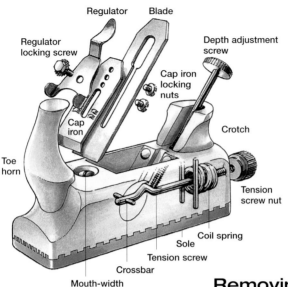

Regulator   Blade

Regulator
locking screw

Depth adjustment
screw

Cap iron
locking
nuts

Cap
iron

Crotch

Toe
horn

Tension
screw nut

Coil spring

Sole

Tension screw

Crossbar

Mouth-width
adjustment screw

▲ Components of a wooden
smoothing plane

opening to suit the thickness of the wood shavings you want to remove. When coarse planing, for example, open the mouth to provide adequate clearance for thick shavings. Close the mouth when taking fine shavings to encourage them to break and curl against the cap iron.

Removing the blade from a wooden plane

Back off the depth adjustment screw by about 10mm (½in), and loosen the tension screw nut at the heel of the plane. Turn the tension screw's crossbar through 90 degrees to release the blade assembly, which includes the cap iron and regulator. To dismantle the assembly for sharpening, remove the two screws at the back of the blade.

Assembling and adjusting a wooden plane

Having sharpened the blade (see pages 101–104), replace the cap iron and lower the assembly into the plane. Pass the crossbar through the slot in the assembly, turning the bar to locate it in its seat in the cap iron, then slightly tighten the tension screw nut.

Adjust the depth screw until the blade protrudes through the mouth; use the regulator to ensure the cutting edge is parallel with the sole. Back off the depth adjuster to the required setting and tighten the tension screw nut.

**ADJUSTING A
SCRUB PLANE**

With the wedge and blade in position, adjust the depth of cut by tapping the top edge of the blade with a mallet. Once you are happy with the setting, tap the wedge home. To release the wedge and blade, strike the toe of the plane.

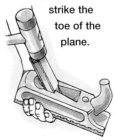

Servicing bench planes

Provided you take reasonable care
of your bench planes, they should
require very little servicing except
for sharpening. Keep planes clean
and well lubricated, and wipe off
occasionally.

Lubricating a sticky sole
Wooden planes rarely require any
form of lubrication, but if you feel
that a metal plane is not gliding
across the work as it should, lightly
rub a stub of candle across the sole.

Preventing shavings jamming
under the cap iron
Check that the back of the blade is
perfectly flat and that there are no
deposits of resin that would prevent
the cap iron from bedding down. If
the blade is bent, lay it on a board
and strike it firmly with a hammer.
Re-dress the leading edge of the
cap iron on an oilstone, honing the
edge flat and at the original angle.

Flattening a warped sole
If your plane seems incapable of
taking a thin shaving, lay a metal
straightedge across the sole to
check that it is not warped. If
necessary, have the plane
reground by a professional.

Flattening a wooden sole on
abrasive paper is much easier.
Remove the blade and, holding the
plane near its centre, rub the sole
back and forth across the paper.

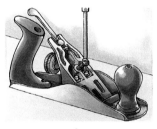

Correcting blade chatter
If your plane vibrates instead of
taking a shaving smoothly, check
that the blade is secure. Tighten the
lever cap screw or, with a wooden
plane, the tension screw nut. If the
fault persists, check there is nothing
trapped behind the blade.

Using bench planes

When setting up a workpiece for planing, inspect the wood to ascertain the general direction of the grain. Planing with the grain is preferable, since planing in the opposite direction tends to tear the wood fibres.

Handling metal planes

Grasp the handle of a metal bench plane with your forefinger extended towards the toe of the tool. Place your free hand on the round knob to hold the toe down onto the work.

Handling wooden smoothing planes

Nestle your hand into the shaped crotch just above the heel of the plane, grasping the body with your fingers and thumb. Use the ergonomic horn to provide downward pressure.

The planing action

Stand beside the bench with your feet apart. Keep your weight on the toe of the plane as you begin the stroke, transferring pressure to the heel to prevent the plane rounding off the work at the far end.

Using a slicing action

It is sometimes easier to smooth irregular grain if you create a slicing action by turning the plane at a slight angle as you slide it forward.

Planing edges

Maintain a square edge by putting pressure on the toe with your thumb, curling your fingers under the plane to act as a guide fence against the side of the work.

Planing a board flat

To plane a board flat, begin by planing at a slight angle across it from two directions. Check the surface with a straightedge (see page 77), then adjust the plane to take thinner shavings and finish with strokes parallel to the edges of the workpiece.

Sharpening tools

A woodworking blade is kept sharp by using abrasive whetstones to wear the metal to a narrow cutting edge. The better-quality natural stones are expensive, but you can get very satisfactory results from cheaper synthetic stones.

Bench stones

Most woodworkers lap and hone their chisel and plane blades on a rectangular bench stone, measuring approximately 200 x 50mm (8 x 2in) and about 25mm (1in) thick. Some woodworkers like to reserve separate stones for each stage of the sharpening process, but for economy, stones with different grades of abrasive are glued back to back. You can also buy similar combinations of natural and synthetic stone.

Oilstones

The majority of natural and man-made sharpening stones are lubricated with a light oil. Novaculite, generally considered to be the finest oilstone available, can be found only in Arkansas, USA. This compact silica crystal occurs naturally in various grades. The coarse, mottled-grey Soft Arkansas stone removes metal quickly and is used for the preliminary shaping of edged tools. The white Hard Arkansas stone puts the honing angle on the cutting edge, which is then refined and polished with Black Arkansas stone. Even finer is the rare translucent variety.

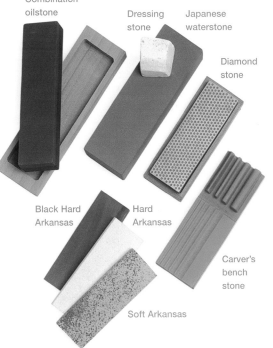

Combination oilstone

Dressing stone

Japanese waterstone

Diamond stone

Black Hard Arkansas

Hard Arkansas

Carver's bench stone

Soft Arkansas

▲ Bench stones

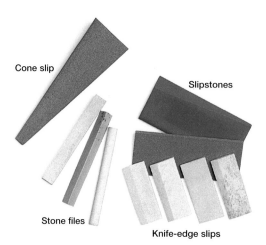

Cone slip

Slipstones

Stone files

Knife-edge slips

▲ Slipstones and stone files

Synthetic oilstones are made from sintered aluminium oxide or silicon carbide. They are far cheaper than their natural equivalents.

Waterstones

Because it is relatively soft and friable, a sharpening stone lubricated with water cuts faster than an equivalent oilstone. Yet this can also make a waterstone vulnerable to accidental damage, especially when honing narrow chisels that could score the surface. Naturally occurring waterstones are so costly that most tool suppliers offer only synthetic varieties, which are almost as efficient.

CARING FOR WHETSTONES

Leave relatively coarse waterstones immersed in water for about five minutes before you use them; finer stones require less time. Keep an oilstone covered to prevent dust sticking to it, and clean the surface regularly. To regrind an oilstone, rub it on an oiled sheet of glass sprinkled with silicon-carbide powder and a waterstone on wet-and-dry paper taped to a sheet of glass.

Diamond stones

Extremely durable coarse- and fine-grade sharpening 'stones' comprise a nickel-plated steel plate that is embedded with monocrystalline diamond particles and bonded to a rigid polycarbonate base. Diamond stones will sharpen steel and carbide tools.

Slipstones and stone files

Small shaped stones are made for sharpening gouges, carving chisels and woodturning tools. Teardrop-section slipstones and tapered cones are the most useful.

Metal lapping plates

Available as alternatives to conventional sharpening stones, oiled steel or cast-iron plates sprinkled with successively finer particles of silicon carbide produce excellent results. For the ultimate cutting edge on steel tools, finish with diamond-grit compound spread on a flat steel plate. Diamond abrasives are also used to hone carbide-tipped tools.

Sharpening blades

Regular sharpening keeps plane blades in optimum condition.

Lapping the back of a blade

Lubricate the stone and hold the blade flat on the surface, bevel-side up. Rub the blade back and forth, maintaining pressure with your fingertips to prevent the blade rocking. Concentrate on the 50mm (2in) of blade directly behind the cutting edge – the rest of the blade can be left with a factory finish. Repeat the process on a fine whetstone until the metal shines.

▲ Lapping the back of a plane blade.

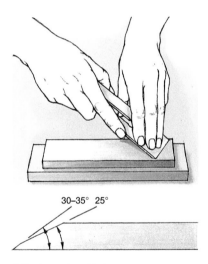

Honing a plane blade

Grasp the blade, bevel-side down, with your index finger extended along one edge. Place the fingertips of your free hand on top of the blade. Place the grinding bevel flat on a lubricated bench stone. Tilt the blade up onto its cutting edge and rub it back and forth along the entire length of the stone to hone the secondary angle.

30–35° 25°

▲ Honing a plane blade.

USING A HONING GUIDE

If you have trouble maintaining an accurate bevel when sharpening chisels and planes, try clamping the blade in a honing guide, a simple jig that holds it at the required angle to a whetstone. A honing guide, of which there are numerous different styles, is convenient for sharpening short spokeshave blades.

Honing a chisel

Sharpen a chisel exactly as described on page 103 – but, because most chisel blades are relatively narrow, move the cutting edge from one side of the bench stone to the other while honing, to avoid wearing a hollow down the middle.

Removing the wire edge

Once you have honed a bevel about 1mm (½in) wide, continue with sharpening the plane blade or chisel on a fine-grade whetstone. Eventually the process wears a 'wire edge' on the blade – a burr you can feel on the back of the blade with your thumb. Remove the burr by lapping the back of the blade on the fine stone, hone the bevel again with a few light strokes, and lap once more until the burr breaks off, leaving a sharp edge. Finally, polish the cutting edge by honing on an extra-fine stone or a leather strop.

Sharpening an out-cannel gouge

To hone the edge of an out-cannel gouge (see page 94), rub the tool crossways on a bench stone, describing a figure-of-eight stroke while rocking the blade from side to side. This brings the whole of the curved edge into contact with the stone and evens out the wear across the stone.

Removing the burr and stropping

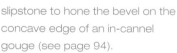

Remove the burr raised on the inside of the blade with a lubricated slipstone. Finally, wrap the stone with a strip of soft leather to strop the edge.

Honing an in-cannel gouge

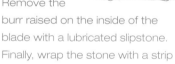

Use a similar slipstone to hone the bevel on the concave edge of an in-cannel gouge (see page 94).

Removing the wire edge

Rub the back of an in-cannel gouge along a lubricated bench stone to remove the wire edge (see left). Keep the back of the gouge flat on the stone while rocking the tool from side to side.

Hand drills and braces

Rugged but lightweight hand drills and ratchet braces are convenient for working 'on site' since they are completely independent of any power source. A brace is especially useful for boring holes up to 50mm (2in) in diameter and can also be used to drive large woodscrews.

No longer featured in every woodworker's tool kit, the hand drill is nevertheless a beautifully engineered tool. Cranking the handle causes the chuck to rotate at relatively high speeds via a system of gear wheels. The chuck will accommodate a wide range of twist drills and dowel bits.

Tool manufacturers still offer a variety of braces, including a special ratchet brace for boring holes through ceiling and floor joists, for plumbing and electrical wiring. An ordinary brace is driven by cranking its frame clockwise while pressure is applied to the round handle at the rear of the tool. The circle described by the moving frame is known as the sweep, and braces are listed in tool catalogues according to the diameter of their sweep.

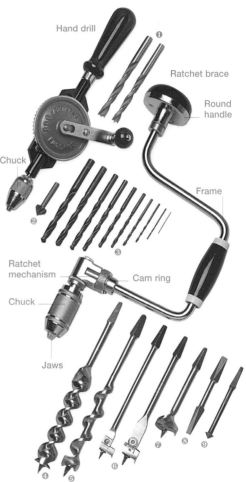

Hand drill

① Ratchet brace

Round handle

Chuck

Frame

②

③

Ratchet mechanism

Cam ring

Chuck

Jaws

▲ The sweep of a brace.

① Dowel bits
② Countersink bit
③ Twist drills
④ Jennings-pattern bit
⑤ Solid-centre auger bit

⑥ Expansive bits
⑦ Centre bit
⑧ Screwdriver bit
⑨ Brace countersink bit

Drill bits

The jaws of a hand drill take a variety of cylindrical twist drills and dowel bits.

Twist drills

Simple twist drills are made with a pair of helical flutes that clear the waste as the drill bores into the wood. Most hand drills take bits up to a maximum diameter of 9mm (⅜in).

Dowel bits

These are wood-boring twist drills with sharp lead points that prevent them wandering off line.

Auger bits

A solid-centre auger bit for a ratchet brace has a single helical twist that brings the waste to the surface and serves to keep the bit on line when boring deep holes.

Expansive bits

An adjustable expansive bit will cut a hole of any size between limits.

Centre bits

Since centre bits are designed to bore relatively shallow holes, they are simpler and therefore cheaper than the equivalent auger bits.

Screwdriver bits

A special double-ended bit converts a brace into a big screwdriver.

Countersink bits

Countersink bits are used to cut tapered recesses for screwheads.

Using a hand drill

Place the tip of the drill bit on the work and gently move the handle back and forth until the bit begins to bite into the wood. Crank the handle at speed to bore a hole to the required depth. Don't apply too much pressure when using small twist drills; the weight of the tool alone will be sufficient to encourage the drill to penetrate the wood.

Boring with a brace

Hold the brace upright with one hand while cranking the frame with the other. To bore horizontally, steady the round handle against your body. To retrieve the bit, lock the ratchet and reverse the action a couple of turns to release the lead screw; then pull on the tool while moving the frame back and forth.

Power drills

The electric drill is the most widely used power tool on the market. Not only is it invaluable for woodwork, it is also an indispensable DIY tool found in nearly every home for general household maintenance tasks.

Mains-powered drills

Drills that run on mains electricity may be relatively heavy and bulky, but they are extremely tough and reliable tools, capable of running more or less continuously for hours on end. Consequently, many woodworkers continue to opt for a mains-powered drill.

Motor size

Manufacturers normally specify the drill's motor as having a power input of so many watts. A 500 to 800W drill capable of producing about 3000rpm is suitable for woodwork.

Drill chucks

Most chucks have three self-centring jaws that grip the shank of a drill bit. Some chucks need tightening with a special toothed key to ensure that the drill bit is held securely by the jaws and will not slip in use, but a great many drills are made with 'keyless' chucks that take a firm grip on the bit simply by turning a cylindrical collar that surrounds the mechanism. Certain drills have an automatic-locking

> ### WATCH OUT!
> • Never wear loose clothing when using a power tool. Tie back loose hair.
> • Wear protective eye shields.
> • Regularly check the flex, casing and plug for signs of wear or damage.
> • Unplug power tools before making adjustments or changing accessories and attachments.

Automatic-locking keyless chuck

All-plastic body

Hammer-action switch

Speed selector/ torque limiter

Depth stop

BOSCH

PSB 750-2 RPE

Gear selector

Reverse-action switch

Secondary handle

Variable-speed trigger

Trigger-lock button

▲ Mains-powered electric drill

▲ Power drill with secondary handle and depth stop.

keyless chuck that can be tightened and loosened with just one hand on the chuck.

Speed selection

Although a few basic drills have a limited range of fixed speeds selected by operating a switch, the majority of drills are variable-speed tools, controlled by the amount of pressure applied to the trigger.

Reverse action

A reverse-action switch changes the direction of rotation so that the drill can be used to extract woodscrews.

Collar size

A drill that has a 43mm-diameter collar (the international standard) directly behind the chuck will fit accessories or attachments made by other manufacturers subscribing to the same system. This gives you the option to buy cheaper or better quality equipment than is made by the drill's manufacturer.

CORDLESS DRILLS

In terms of performance, most modern cordless drills compare well with mains-powered drills. Cordless drills are also comparatively lightweight and make less noise.

Most cordless drills have a chuck capacity of between 10 and 13mm (⅜ and ½in) but, using specialized bits, will bore holes up to 30mm (1¼in) in diameter in wood. Power drills fitted with hammer action (combi drills) will bore into masonry as well as wood. The majority of cordless drills have keyless chucks.

Speed selector/ torque limiter

Gear selector

Keyless chuck

Trigger

Reverse-action switch

Screwdriver bit

Battery pack

Power drill bits

Most power drills have a chuck capacity – the maximum size of drill-bit shank that the chuck will accommodate – of 10 or 13mm (⅜ or ½in). The shank size of an ordinary twist drill or dowel bit corresponds exactly to the size of hole that particular bit will bore.

Twist drills

Although twist drills are designed for metalwork, they also serve as good general-purpose woodboring bits. Carbon-steel twist drills are perfectly adequate for woodwork, but since you will almost certainly want to drill metal at some time, it is worth investing in the more expensive high-speed-steel bits. Twist drills ranging from 13 to 25mm (½ to 1in) in diameter are made with reduced shanks to fit standard power-drill chucks.

Dowel bits

The dowel bit is a twist drill that has a centre point, to prevent it wandering off line, and two spurs that cut a clean-edged hole.

Spade bits

These are inexpensive drill bits made for power-drilling large holes from 6 to 38mm (¼ to 1½in) in diameter. A long lead point makes for positive location even when drilling at an angle to the face of the work.

Masonry drills

Masonry drills are steel twist drills with a brazed tungsten-carbide tip designed to bore into brick, stone or concrete.

Percussion drills

These masonry drills have a shatter-proof tip designed to withstand the vibration produced by hammer action.

❶ Reduced-shank twist drill
❷ Spade bit
❸ Forstner bit

MUST KNOW

Working with twist drills

● Twist drills are not easy to locate on the dead centre of a hole – so, particularly when drilling hardwoods, it pays to mark the centre of the hole first, using a metalworking punch.

● To avoid splintering the wood, take the pressure off the drill as the bit emerges from the far side of the work.

● Keep twist drills sharp and, before use, pick out any wood dust that has become packed into the flutes.

① Countersink bit
② Plug cutter
③ Drill-and-countersink bit
④ Drill-and-counterbore bit

Forstner bits

Forstner bits leave exceptionally clean flat-bottomed holes up to 50mm (2in) in diameter. These bits will not be deflected even by wild grain or knots.

Countersink bits

Similar to the countersink bits made for hand drills and braces, these drill bits are used to make tapered recesses for the heads of woodscrews. Centre the bit on a clearance hole bored in the wood, and run the power drill at a high speed for a clean finish.

VERTICAL DRILL STAND

A vertical stand converts a portable power drill into a serviceable pillar drill. Pulling down on the feed lever lowers the drill bit into the work. When you release the feed lever, a spring automatically returns the drill to its starting position.

Drill-and-countersink bits

These specialized bits cut a pilot hole, clearance hole and countersink for a woodscrew in one operation.

Drill-and-counterbore bits

Instead of cutting a tapered recess for a screw head, this type of bit leaves a neat hole that allows the screw to be driven below the face of the workpiece.

Plug cutters

Driving a plug cutter into side grain cuts a cylindrical plug of wood to match the hole left by a drill-and-counterbore bit. Cut plugs from timber that closely matches the colour and grain pattern of the work.

Screwdriver bits

Different bits are needed for slotted and cross-head screws. Locate the screwdriver bit in the screw slot before switching on.

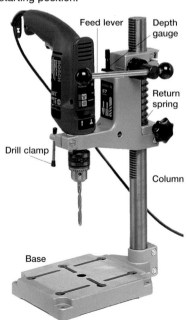

Feed lever

Depth gauge

Return spring

Drill clamp

Column

Base

Screwdrivers

Nowadays, many woodworkers use a power screwdriver, but in reality you need no more than a handful of basic screwdrivers for driving simple straight-slot and cross-head screws.

Cabinet screwdriver

The standard, general-purpose woodworking screwdriver has a relatively large, oval-shape plastic or wooden grip that fits comfortably in the palm of the hand. The traditional flat tip may be ground from a cylindrical shaft or flared and then ground back to a tapered tip. The tip must fit the screw slot snugly, so it is worth investing in a range of screwdriver sizes.

Cross-head screwdriver

Traditional-pattern woodscrews and modern, fast-action, double-helical screws are both made with cross shape slots to improve the grip between the screwdriver tip and screw. The matching screwdrivers are made with pointed tips ground with four flutes.

Screwdriver bits

Straight-slot and cross-head bits are available for use with power screwdrivers or variable-speed electric drills.

Offset screwdriver

A cranked bar of metal ground at each end to form a straight or cross-head tip. It is ideal for inserting knock-down joints that would be inaccessible using a conventional screwdriver.

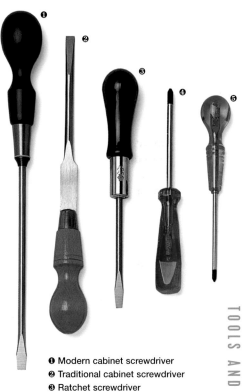

❶ Modern cabinet screwdriver
❷ Traditional cabinet screwdriver
❸ Ratchet screwdriver
❹ Posidriv screwdriver
❺ Phillips screwdriver

Woodworking cramps

Interlocking woodworking joints are designed to ensure optimum contact area between components, so that they bond well with adhesive. The main purpose of using cramps is to help assemble the workpiece and hold the parts together while the glue sets.

Sash cramps are used for assembling large frames, panels and carcasses. A sash cramp has a screw-adjustable jaw attached to one end of a flat steel bar.

Fast-action cramps are designed for speedy adjustment to fit the size of the work. Various versions are available.

The G-cramp is an excellent general purpose cramp that is often used to hold wood to a bench while you work on it. Usually made from cast iron, the frame forms a fixed jaw.

A handscrew is a traditional cramp with wide wooden jaws that can be set to apply even pressure over a broad area. It is particularly useful when assembling out-of-square frames or for clamping tapered workpieces.

A mitre cramp holds glued mitre joints at right angles, preventing the components from slipping while reinforcing nails are inserted.

❶ Pipe cramp
❷ Sash cramp
❸ Fast-action cramp
❹ G-cramp
❺ Long-reach G-cramp
❻ Short fast-action cramp
❼ Handscrew
❽ Mitre cramp

Woodworking adhesives

Today woodworkers are able to choose from a range of excellent adhesives with different properties, and most of them are capable of forming a bond so tough that the glue line is stronger than the surrounding wood fibres.

Animal glues

The traditional woodworking glue is still made using animal skins and bone to provide the protein that gives its adhesive quality. Although once the staple woodwork adhesive, animal glue is now rarely used except for hand-laying veneers, where its thermoplastic quality is especially advantageous.

▲ Animal glue 'pearls' are dissolved in water in a jacketed glue pot.

Hot-melt glues

Hot-melt glue is sold in the form of cylindrical sticks for application using a special electrically heated 'gun'. This type of adhesive is convenient to use and sets within seconds, which makes it ideal for constructing mock-ups and jigs.

PVA adhesives

One of the cheapest and most convenient woodworking adhesives is 'white glue', a ready-made emulsion of polyvinyl acetate (PVA) suspended in water that sets when the water evaporates or is absorbed into the wood.

An excellent general-purpose non-toxic wood glue, it has an almost indefinite shelf life so long as it is kept in reasonably warm conditions. Although the tough semi-flexible glue line can creep, this doesn't usually happen except when a joint is subjected to stress over a prolonged period.

▼ Hot-melt glue gun and glue sticks

TOOLS AND TECHNIQUES

113

APPLYING GLUES

Unless they are sold with an applicator, you can spread adhesives with a brush, flat stick or roller. When preparing glue, always follow the manufacturer's recommendations.

Glue brush
A wire bridle stiffens the bristles of a glue brush. It can be removed when the bristles wear down.

Glue syringe
Use a plastic syringe to apply an exact amount of woodworking adhesive when you need to glue inaccessible joints.

Glue brush

Glue syringe

114

MUST KNOW

Surface preparation
● For glue to be effective, joining surfaces must be well prepared: clean, grease-free, flat and smooth.
● Roughing surfaces to provide a better key is not recommended for wood joints.

Moisture content
The moisture content of the wood can affect the quality of a joint. If it is more than about 20 per cent, some glues may never set satisfactorily.

Urea-formaldehyde adhesives

Urea-formaldehyde glue is an excellent water-resistant gap-filling adhesive that cures by chemical reaction. You can buy it in a powdered form which, once it has been mixed with water, is applied to both mating surfaces.

Resorcinol-resin glues

Similar in many ways to urea-formaldehyde adhesives, resorcinol-resin glue is completely waterproof and weather-resistant. It is a two-part glue comprising a resin and a separate hardener.

Polyurethane glues

These waterproof glues are able to form a particularly strong joint in difficult situations, especially when you are trying to join end grain to cross grain. End-grain fibres tend to absorb water-based glues and swell, then shrink when the moisture dries out. This can sometimes weaken the joint. Polyurethane glues expand as they cure, which overcomes the problem. Once they have set, these glues neither contract nor expand and can be stained and sanded.

Contact adhesives

A contact adhesive is spread as a thin layer on both mating surfaces. After the glue has set, the two components are brought together and the bond is instant. Modified versions allow the positions of the components to be adjusted until pressure is applied with a block of wood or a roller, causing the glue to bond. This type of adhesive is used extensively for gluing melamine laminates to kitchen worktops.

▲ Spread contact adhesive using the applicator supplied with the product.

Epoxy-resin adhesives

Epoxy adhesive is a synthetic two-part glue consisting of a resin and a hardener, normally mixed in equal proportions just before application. The most common form of epoxy glue is a general-purpose adhesive – sold in tubes – for joining diverse materials. As it is relatively thick, it is not really suitable for woodwork. However, you can buy liquid versions of the adhesive, made for gluing wood.

Epoxy glues cure by chemical reaction to form a strong transparent glue line. Standard epoxy adhesives take a few hours to set hard, but fast-setting glues are also available.

Cyanoacrylate glues

The cyanoacrylates – 'super glues' – come close to being universal adhesives. They bond a great many materials, including human skin – so take care when handling them and keep a proprietary super-glue solvent in your workshop.

Super glues must be used sparingly. Most are thin liquids, but a gel type is also available. They are commonly used by woodturners and carvers for making fast repairs.

want to know **more?**

Take it to the next level...

Go to...
▶ **Filling cracks & holes** – pages 148–50
▶ **Power sanding** – pages 157–61
▶ **Stains and dyes** – page 165–71

Other sources
▶ **www.toolpost.co.uk**
   visit The Toolpost, which specializes in the supply of quality tools and equipment for woodturners, carvers and woodworkers
▶ **Qualification**
   consider taking a City & Guilds Diploma in Basic Woodworking Skills. Visit www.city-and-guilds.co.uk for information on all C&G courses

making

joints

Joinery – the making of joints – is at the very heart of woodworking. Without the means to connect pieces of wood, the construction of furniture and many other wooden objects would be impossible. There are lots of different types of joint, some more complex than others, with many varied purposes.

Butt joints

The butt joint is the simplest of the various joints, where one member meets another with no interlocking elements cut into the parts. It is not a strong joint, and is often reinforced in some way. Right-angled butt joints are used in the construction of light frames and small boxes. The jointing ends may be square-cut or mitred.

Square-ended butt joint

It is possible to make flat frames and simple box structures utilizing square-cut corner joints. Since glue alone is rarely sufficient to make a sturdy butt joint, hold the parts together with fine nails or glued blocks of wood.

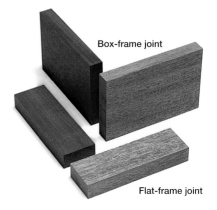

Box-frame joint

Flat-frame joint

1 Cutting the joint

Mark out each piece of wood to length, using a knife and try square to mark the shoulders of the joint on all faces. Hold the work against a bench hook (see opposite page), and saw down each shoulder, keeping to the waste side of the marked line.

2 Squaring the ends

For all but the most basic work, trim the ends square to form a neat butt joint, using a bench plane and shooting board (see opposite page). Set the plane for a fine cut, and lubricate the running surfaces of the shooting board with a white candle or wax polish.

Reinforcing a butt joint

For additional strength, drive nails at an angle into the wood as shown below, or glue a corner block on the inside for a neater finish.

MAKING JOINTS

▲ Cutting the joint.

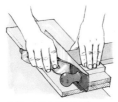

▲ Squaring the ends.

▲ Reinforcing a square-ended butt joint.

Mitred butt joint

The classic joint for picture frames, the mitred butt joint makes a neat right-angle corner without visible end grain. Cutting wood at 45 degrees produces a relatively large surface area of tangentially cut grain that glues well. For lightweight frames, just add glue and set the joint in a mitre cramp.

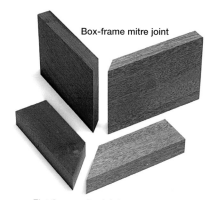

Box-frame mitre joint

Accurate mitre cutting

Before you pick up a saw, always ensure that the mitre is exactly half the joint angle, or the joint will be gappy. In addition, use well-seasoned timber or a gap may open up on the inside of the joint as the wood shrinks.

Flat-frame mitre joint

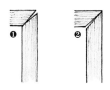

▲ Gaps in mitres may be caused by
❶ inaccurate cutting ❷ shrinkage.

MAKING A BENCH HOOK

Cut a baseboard about 250 x 200mm (10 x 8in) from close-grained hardwood such as beech or maple, 18mm (¾in) thick. Cut two stop blocks 150mm (6in) long and 38mm (1½in) wide. Glue and dowel the blocks flush with the ends of the baseboard, on opposite faces. Inset the blocks by 25mm (1in) from each long edge; this enables the guide to be used by left- or right-handed woodworkers.

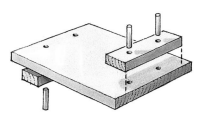

MAKING A SHOOTING BOARD

● Cut two boards 600mm (2ft) long, one from 225 x 25mm (9 x 1in) close-grained hardwood and the other from 150 x 25mm (6 x 1in) hardwood. Glue them face to face to form a step.
● For a square-cutting version, glue and dowel a stop block at one end, at right angles to the stepped edge.
● For a mitre shooting board, fix two stop blocks in the centre at 45 degrees to the stepped edge.
● Fix a batten to the underside for clamping the jig in a vice. Alternatively, leave the underside flat and clamp the jig between bench stops.

▲ Cutting the joint.

▲ Trimming the joint.

▲ Trimming a wide board.

1 Cutting the joint

On each piece of wood, mark the sloping shoulder of the joint, using a knife and mitre square. Extend the marked line across the adjacent faces with a try square. To remove the waste, either follow the marked lines by eye or use a mitre box to guide the saw blade.

2 Trimming the joint

Hold the work on a mitre shooting board and trim each cut end with a sharp bench plane, bringing the mitres to a tidy finish.

USING A MITRE SAW

It pays to use a special jig called a mitre saw to cut larger pieces of wood or moulded sections of framing. The workpiece can be held on edge or flat on the bed of the tool. The saw guide, which can be set to any angle, guarantees accurate joints.

Trimming a wide board

Since it is impossible to mitre a wide piece of wood on a shooting board, clamp the work upright in a bench vice and trim the end grain with a finely set block plane. To prevent splitting, back up the work with a piece of scrap timber.

Reinforcing mitred joints

The easiest way to reinforce a mitred joint is to drive nails through the joint after the glue has set.

Alternatively, veneer splines, or plywood tongues or keys may be used.

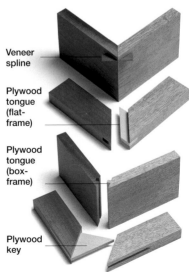

Veneer spline

Plywood tongue (flat-frame)

Plywood tongue (box-frame)

Plywood key

▲ Reinforcing mitred joints.

Edge-to-edge joints

Edge joints are used to join narrow boards together to make up a large panel, such as a table top. With a modern wood glue, even a plain butt joint can be adequate.

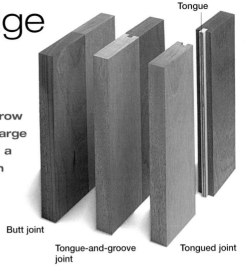

Tongue

Butt joint

Tongue-and-groove joint

Tongued joint

Edge-to-edge butt joint

Timber selection is as important as good edge-to-edge joints when making a wide panel from solid wood. To ensure that the panel will remain flat, try to use quarter-sawn wood – that is, with the endgrain growth rings running perpendicular to the face side of each board. Before you set to work, number each board and mark the face side.

Planing edges square

With the face sides on the outside, set both boards back-to-back and level in a vice. Plane the edges straight and square, using the longest bench plane you can find.

Checking for straight edges

It is vital that the edges are straight if you intend to use a rubbed joint; check them using a straightedge.

Matching edges

It is good practice to keep the edges as square as possible.

However, provided boards have been planed as a pair, they will fit together and produce a flat surface, even when the edges are not exactly square.

Clamping joints

Before adding glue, set prepared boards in sash cramps to check that the joints fit snugly. Use at least three cramps, alternated as shown, to counter any bowing.

▲ Planing edges square.

▲ Checking for straight edges.

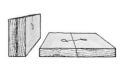

▲ Matching edges.

▲ Clamping the joint.

MAKING RUBBED JOINTS

Small, accurately cut edge-to-edge joints can be assembled without cramps. Apply glue to both parts and rub them together, squeezing out air and adhesive until atmospheric pressure holds the surfaces in contact while the glue sets.

Tongue-and-groove joint

Use a combination plane to cut a tongue-and-groove joint by hand. Clamp the work in a bench vice, face-side towards you. Adjust the fence until the cutter is centred on the edge of the work. Adjust the plane's depth stop to cut a tongue of the required size, and plane to form the tongue. Select a ploughing cutter to match the width of the tongue, and fit into the plane. Adjust the fence while sitting the cutter on top of the tongue, set the depth stop to cut a groove slightly deeper than the tongue. Clamp the uncut board in the vice and cut the groove.

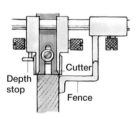

▲ Set the plane to cut the tongue.

▲ Cutting the tongue.

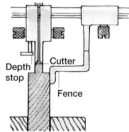

▲ Adjust the plane to cut the groove.

A LOOSE TONGUE

A loose tongue has three advantages over using an integral one: it avoids decreasing the width of the boards; it gives the joint marginally greater strength; and a simple plough plane can be used to cut the grooves. Plane a groove down the centre of each board and insert a separate tongue made from plywood or solid timber (ideally cross-grained). Glue one groove and tap the tongue into it, then brush glue into the other groove and assemble the joint in cramps as described above.

Lap joint

A basic lap joint is only marginally strong than a straightforward butt joint, but it is an improvement in appearance, since most of the end grain is concealed.

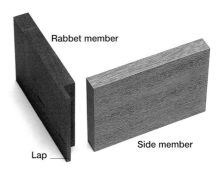

Rabbet member

Side member

Lap

1 Marking out the rabbet

Cut and plane both members square. Adjust a marking gauge to about one-quarter of the thickness of the rabbet member, and scribe a line across the end grain, working from the face side. Continue the line on both edges, down to the level of the shoulder.

2 Marking the shoulder

Set a cutting gauge to match the thickness of the side member, and scribe a shoulder line parallel to the end grain on the back of the rabbet member. Continue the shoulder line across both edges to meet the lines already scribed.

SCARF JOINT

A form of lap and mitre joint in one, this is used to join wood end to end. You can saw or plane the long shallow tapers, which give a large gluing area. Make the length of the tapers at least four times the thickness of the wood.

3 Cutting the joint

Clamp the rabbet member upright in a vice. Following the line scribed across the end grain, saw down to the shoulder line. Lay the work face-down on a bench hook and cut down the shoulder line with a tenon saw to remove the waste. Make a neat joint by cleaning up the rabbet with a shoulder plane.

4 Assembling the joint

Glue and clamp the joint, then drive panel pins or small lost-head nails through the side member. Sink the pins with a nail set and fill the holes.

▲ Marking out the rabbet.　▲ Marking the shoulder.

▲ Cutting the joint.　▲ Assembling the joint.

Dowel joints

A dowel joint is nothing more than a butt joint reinforced with short wooden pegs – but, despite this simplicity, it is virtually as strong as a mortise-and-tenon. It is, however, considerably easier to make.

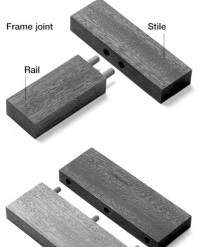

Frame joint

Stile

Rail

Edge-to-edge joint

Carcass joint

▲ Dowel joints

Dowelled frame joints

Frames made with dowelled butt joints are surprisingly strong. In most cases, two dowels per joint are sufficient.

Saw each component to length and trim the ends of the rail square as described for making a square-ended butt joint (see page 118). Leave the stile or leg of a corner joint overlong until the joint is finished.

Clamp the two components in a vice with their joining surfaces flush. Using a try square, draw the centre of each dowel hole across both components, then scribe a line centrally on each one with a

DOWELS

If you need a few dowels only, cut them from a length of dowel rod. Steady the rod on a bench hook and cut off short sections with a fine-tooth saw. Chamfer each dowel with a file, and saw a single glue slot.

Ready-made dowels are manufactured from tough short-grain woods, such as ramin.

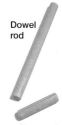

Dowel rod

Prepared dowel

Fluted dowel

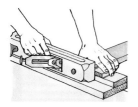

▲ Trimming the rail square.

▲ Marking the joint.

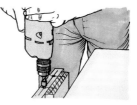

▲ Boring the dowel holes.

marking gauge. Bore the dowel holes where the lines cross.

Place the point of a dowel bit on the marked centre and bore each hole in turn. Unless you are using a dowelling jig or a drill stand, it pays to have someone nearby who can tell you when the drill bit is vertical.

OTHER MARKING TECHNIQUES

Using centre points

For greater accuracy in marking out dowel joints, draw the centre points on the end of the rail only, then drive in panel pins where the lines cross. Cut off the pin heads with pliers, leaving short 'spikes' projecting from the end grain.

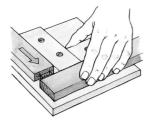

Next, lay the leg or stile on its side and press the end of the rail firmly against it, leaving two pinholes that mark the hole centres exactly. A simple right-angle jig keeps the components aligned.

Edge-to-edge dowel joint

When constructing a wide solid-wood panel, you can make a particularly strong joint between boards by inserting a dowel every 225 to 300mm (9 to 12in).

Clamp adjacent boards back-to-back in a vice and mark the dowel centres, using a try square and pencil. Scribe a line down the centre of each board with a marking gauge.

If possible, have a helper stand nearby, to tell you when the drill is upright as you bore each hole where the marked lines cross.

Each hole should be slightly deeper than half the length of the dowel. To enable you to drill consistently deep holes, fit a plastic guide onto the drill bit. Depth stops are fairly inexpensive, but if you prefer, bind a strip of adhesive tape around the drill bit to mark the appropriate level.

▲ Marking an edge-to-edge joint.

▲ Boring the holes.

MAKING JOINTS

125

DOWELLING JIGS

It's worth acquiring a dowelling jig for a project that requires a number of identical dowel joints. The jig not only guides the bit to bore perfectly vertical holes, it also dispenses with the need to mark out each and every joint separately. With better jigs, you can mark out wide boards for cabinet work as well as rails and stiles. The jig shown here has a fixed head or fence from which measurements are taken, and a sliding fence that clamps the jig to the workpiece.

Sliding fence

Drill-bit guide

Fixed head

▲ Drilling the end grain for a right-angle butt joint.

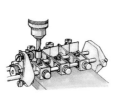

▲ Drilling matching holes in the other piece.

▲ Drilling the holes for a T-joint.

▲ Dowelling a mitred carcass joint.

Carcass butt joints

For a carcass with butt joints reinforced with multiple dowels, use a dowelling jig with extra-long slide rods and additional drill-bit guides.

1 Dowelling a corner joint

For a right-angle butt joint, drill the end grain first. Set the jig's side fences to position the dowel holes centrally on the thickness of the workpiece, and adjust the drill-bit guides to space the dowels 50 to 75mm (2 to 3in) apart.

2 Drilling matching holes

Without changing any settings, invert the jig and clamp it to the inside of the other component, with the side fences butted against the end grain and the fixed head against the face edge.

Making a T-joint

To make a T-joint, drill the end grain as described above; remove the side fences and clamp the jig across the matching component.

Dowelling a mitred carcass joint

To make a dowel-reinforced mitre joint, assemble a jig similar to that used for a right-angle butt joint, and clamp it to the bevelled end of the workpiece. Adjust the drill-bit guides to position the dowels towards the lower edge of the bevel. Having drilled the dowel holes, transfer the jig to the other mitred board and drill matching holes.

Bridle joints

Used exclusively for frame construction, the bridle joint is similar in appearance to a mortise-and-tenon, though in most circumstances it would not be as strong.

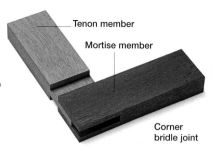

Tenon member

Mortise member

Corner bridle joint

Corner bridle joint

A corner bridle joint is adequate for relatively lightweight frames, provided they are not subjected to sideways pressure.

1 Marking out the shoulders

Mark square shoulders all round each tenon member using a marking knife, but apply light pressure across both edges. Mark out the mortise member similarly, but this time use a pencil.

2 Scribing the tenon

Set the points of a mortise gauge to one-third the thickness of the wood, and adjust the tool's stock to centre the points on the edge of the work. Scribe the width of the tenon on both edges and across the end.

3 Marking out the open mortise

Use the same gauge to mark the sides of the open mortise, then take a marking knife and score the short shoulders at the base of the mortise, between the gauged lines.

4 Cutting the open mortise

Select a drill bit that approximates the width of the mortise, and bore a hole into the waste wood just above the shoulder line on opposite sides of the joint. Set the wood in a vice and saw on the waste side of both gauged lines. Chisel the shoulder square.

5 Cutting the tenon

With the work clamped in a vice, saw both sides of the tenon down to the shoulder. Lay the workpiece on its side on a bench hook and saw each shoulder line to remove the waste wood.

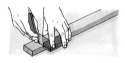

▲ Marking out the shoulder.

▲ Scribing the tenon.

▲ Tenon and mortise marking complete.

▲ Cutting the open mortise.

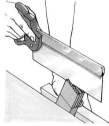

▲ Cutting the tenon.

Mitred bridle joint

The mitred bridle is cut in a similar way to the conventional corner joint, but is a more attractive alternative for framing, because end grain appears on one edge only.

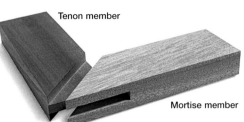

Tenon member

Mortise member

1 Marking the joint

Cut the components exactly to length. Mark the width of the parts on each end and square the shoulders all round, using a try square and pencil. Mark the sloping face of the mitre on both sides of each component with a knife and mitre square.

2 Gauging the tenon and open mortise

Set the pins of a mortise gauge to one-third the thickness of the wood, and adjust the stock to centralize the pair of pins on the edge of the work. Scribe the width of the tenon on the inside edge and across the end grain of the appropriate member. On the mortise member, scribe similar lines across the end and on both edges.

3 Cutting the open mortise

Cut out the waste from the mortise as described for a conventional corner bridle joint, then hold the work on a bench hook and saw down the marked line to mitre both cheeks of the joint. If the mitres are not perfect, shave them with a block plane.

4 Cutting the tenon

Clamp the tenon member at an angle in a vice and saw down to the mitred shoulder on both sides of the tenon; keep the saw blade just to the waste side of the line. Holding the work on a bench hook, saw along both mitred shoulders to remove the waste. If necessary, trim the mitred surfaces with a shoulder plane.

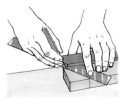

▲ Marking the joint.

▲ Gauging the tenon and open mortise.

▲ Cutting the open mortise.

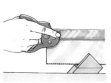

▲ Cutting the tenon.

T-bridle joint

The T-bridle serves as an intermediate support for a frame.

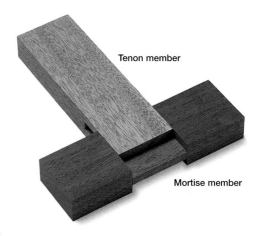

Tenon member

Mortise member

1 Marking the shoulders
Mark the width of the mortise member on the tenon member, using a marking knife to score square shoulders all round.

2 Gauging the joint
Set the pins of a mortise gauge to one-third the thickness of the wood, and adjust the stock to centre the pair of pins on the edge of the workpiece. Scribe parallel lines between the marked shoulders on the tenon member, then mark similar lines on the end and both edges of the mortise member.

3 Cutting the open mortise
Cut the mortise as described for a corner bridle joint. Alternatively, saw down both sides of the open mortise with a tenon saw, then use a coping saw to remove the waste, cutting as close to the shoulder as possible.

4 Cutting the tenon member
On both sides of the tenon member, saw the shoulders down to the gauged lines, then make three or four similar saw cuts in between. With the work held firmly, chop out the waste with a mallet and chisel, working from each edge towards the middle. Having assembled the joint, allow the glue to set.

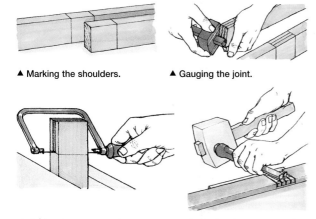

▲ Marking the shoulders.

▲ Gauging the joint.

▲ Cutting the open mortise.

▲ Cutting the tenon member.

TABLE-LEG VERSION

When joining a square leg to a table underframe, make the 'tenon' about two-thirds the thickness of the rail. Offset the open mortise so that a slightly overhanging table top can conceal the leg's end grain.

Housing joints

A housing is a groove cut across the grain. When used as a joint, it houses the end of a board – most frequently a fixed shelf or dividing panel. The housing can be stopped short of the front edge of the work, but for less important work the joint may emerge as a through housing.

Side panel

Shelf

Through housing joint

Through housing joint

This simple through joint shows on the front edges of side panels. It is suitable for rough shelving, or for cupboards with lay-on doors that cover the front edges. If you plan to lip the boards, it is best to apply the lippings first to make it easier to plane them flush.

1 Marking the face of the side panel

Measure the width of the housing

from the shelf, then score the two lines across the workpiece, using a try square and marking knife.

2 Marking the edges

Square the same lines onto the edges of the panel, then scribe a line between them, using a marking gauge set to about 6mm (¼in).

3 Sawing the housing shoulders

To make it easier to locate a saw across a wide panel, take a chisel and pare a shallow V-shape groove up to the marked line on both sides of the housing, then use a tenon saw to cut each shoulder down to the lines scribed on each edge.

4 Removing the waste

Pare out the waste from a narrow panel with a chisel, working from each side towards the middle.

▲ Marking the face of the side panel.

▲ Marking the edges.

▲ Sawing the housing shoulders.

▲ Removing the waste.

Dovetail housing joint

When cutting this joint by hand, incorporate a single dovetail along one side of the housing. Double-sided dovetails are best cut with a power router. Since the shelf member must be slid into place from one end of the housing, the joint needs to be cut accurately.

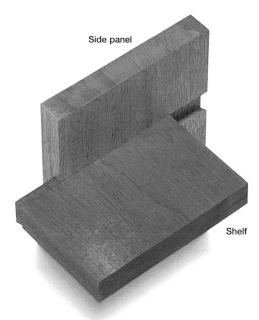

Side panel

Shelf

1 Marking the shoulder

Set a cutting gauge to about one-third the thickness of the wood and score a shoulder line on the underside of the shelf. Using a try square and pencil, continue the line across both edges.

2 Marking the dovetail angle

Set a sliding bevel to a dovetail angle (see pages 79–80), and mark the slope of the joint, running from the bottom corner to the marks drawn on both edges.

3 Paring the slope

Saw along the shoulder line, down to the base of the slope, then pare out the waste with a chisel. To help keep the angle constant, use a shaped block of wood to guide the blade.

4 Cutting the housing

Mark out the housing as described opposite, and use the sliding bevel to mark the dovetail on both edges of the panel. Saw both shoulders,

using a bevelled block of wood to guide the saw blade when cutting the dovetail. Remove the waste with a router plane, or use a bevel-edge chisel to clear the undercut.

▲ Marking the shoulder.

▲ Marking the dovetail angle.

▲ Paring the slope.

▲ Cutting the housing.

Stopped housing joint

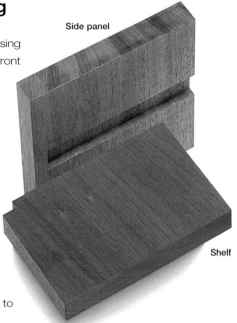

Side panel

Shelf

For decorative effect, the housing is often stopped short of the front edge of the side panel by about 9 to 12mm (⅜ to ½in). Occasionally, the shelf is also cut short, fitting the housing exactly – useful when making a cupboard with inset doors. Generally, however, the front edge of the shelf is notched so that its front edge finishes flush with the side panel. The instructions below explain how to cut the joint with handtools, but you could use a power router to cut a stopped housing.

1 Notching the shelf

Set a marking gauge to the planned depth of the housing, and use it to mark the notch on the front corner of the shelf. Cut the notch with a tenon saw.

▲ Notching the shelf.

▲ Marking the housing.

▲ Cutting the stopped end.

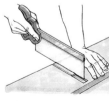

▲ Sawing the housing.

2 Marking the housing

Use the notched shelf to mark the dimensions of the housing, then score the lines across the side panel with a try square and marking knife. Scribe the stopped end of the housing with a marking gauge.

3 Cutting the stopped end

To provide clearance for sawing the housing, first drill out the waste at the stopped end and trim the shoulders square with a chisel.

4 Sawing the housing

Saw along the scored shoulders down to the base of the housing, then pare out the waste from the back edge with a chisel, or use a router plane.

Barefaced housing joint

The barefaced housing joint is a variation on the basic lap joint, adapted for making box-frame or cabinet corners. The housing should be no deeper than about one-quarter the thickness of the wood, and about the same in width.

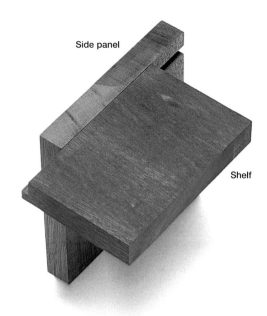

Side panel

Shelf

1 Marking the housing

Cut and plane square the ends of both components. Set a cutting gauge to the thickness of the horizontal member, and lightly scribe the bottom edge of the housing across the side panel and down both edges. Reset the gauge and scribe the top edge of the housing in the same way.

2 Marking the tongue

Using the gauge with the same setting, mark the tongue on the end and down both edges of the horizontal member, working from the face side.

3 Marking the rabbet shoulder

Reset the gauge to about one-third the thickness of the side panel, and mark the rabbet shoulder line across the face side and down both edges of the horizontal member. Form the rabbet by removing the waste with a saw and cleaning up the rough edges with a shoulder plane.

4 Cutting the housing

Mark the depth of the housing on the edges of the side panel and remove the waste with a saw and chisel, as described for a through housing joint (see page 130).

▲ Marking the housing.

▲ Marking the tongue.

▲ Marking the rabbet shoulder.

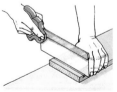

▲ Cutting the housing.

Halving joints

Halving joints are employed exclusively for framing, using wood of equal thickness for both components of the joint. These joints are easy to cut with handtools or with a machine.

Divider

Rail

Cross halving joint

Cross halving joint

With a cross halving joint, both halves of the joint are identical. Although the joint is equally strong whichever way the components run, convention dictates that the vertical member or divider appears to run through. In reality, however, half the thickness is removed from each piece of wood.

1 Marking the shoulders

Lay both components side-by-side and score the shoulder lines across them, using a try square and marking knife. Continue both sets of marked lines halfway down each edge.

2 Marking the depth of the joint

Set a marking gauge to exactly half the thickness of the wood, and scribe a line between the shoulders marked on the edges of both components.

3 Cutting the joint

Saw halfway through both pieces of wood on the waste side of each shoulder line. Divide the waste wood between the shoulders with one or two additional saw cuts.

4 Chopping out the waste

Clamp the work in a vice and chisel out the waste, working from each side towards the middle of each component. Pare the bottom of each resulting recess flat with a chisel.

▲ Marking the shoulders.

▲ Marking the depth of the joint.

▲ Cutting the joint.

▲ Chopping out the waste.

Corner halving joint

You can construct a simple framework, using a halving joint at each corner. However, since this type of joint relies almost entirely on glue for strength, you may need to reinforce it with woodscrews or hardwood dowels. The mitred halving joint is a refined version, but it has even less gluing area.

Corner
halving joint

Mitred halving joint

1 Marking the basic halving joint

Lay the components side by side, and mark the shoulder line across both of them. Continue the lines down each edge.

2 Gauging the depth

Set a marking gauge to half the thickness of the wood and scribe a line up both edges and across the end grain. Remove the waste with a tenon saw, cutting downwards from the end grain, followed by sawing across the shoulder.

3 Marking a mitred corner

Mark and cut one component as described above, then cut the lap to 45 degrees. Score the angled shoulder line across the face of the second component, using a knife and mitre square, then scribe the centre line up the inner edge and across the end grain.

4 Cutting the angled shoulder

Clamp the work at an angle in a vice and saw on the waste side of the centre line, down to the shoulder. Lay the work on a bench hook, and remove the waste by sawing down the shoulder line.

▲ Marking the basic housing joint.

▲ Gauging the depth.

▲ Marking a mitred corner.

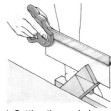

▲ Cutting the angled shoulder.

T-halving joint

A means of joining an intermediate support to a frame, the T-halving joint is a combination of the cross-halving and corner-halving versions.

1 Marking out the joint

Taking the dimensions from the relevant components, score the shoulder lines with a knife and try square, and scribe the depth of the joint on each workpiece with a marking gauge.

2 Cutting the recess

Chisel out the waste from between the shoulders. Use the long edge of the chisel blade to check that the bottom of the recess is flat.

3 Sawing the lap

Saw down to the shoulder, keeping the saw blade just to the waste side of the gauged line. You may find it easier to keep the cut vertical if you tilt the work away from you while sawing down one edge. Turn the work round and saw down the other edge, then finish off by sawing squarely down to the shoulder.

4 Removing the waste

With the wood resting on a bench hook, saw down the shoulder line to remove the waste. If necessary, trim the shoulder square with a chisel or shoulder plane (see page 96).

▲ Marking out the joint.

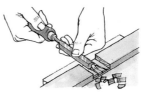

▲ Cutting the recess.

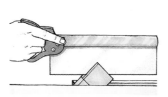

▲ Sawing the lap.

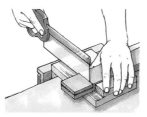

▲ Removing the waste.

Dovetail housing joint

Incorporate a dovetail to increase the strength of a T-halving joint. This stronger joint is only marginally more difficult to make than the standard square-shoulder joint and worth the effort.

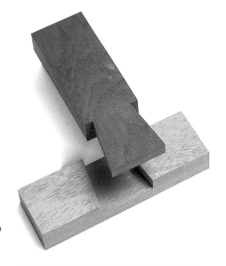

1 Marking the lap dovetail

Having marked out and cut a lap in the conventional manner, use a template (see box, right) and knife to mark the dovetail on the workpiece.

2 Shaping the lap dovetail

Saw the short shoulders on both sides of the lap, then pare away the waste with a chisel to form the sloping sides of the dovetail.

3 Marking and cutting the recess

Using the dovetailed lap as a template, score the shoulders of the recess on the cross member. Mark the depth of the recess with a marking gauge (see pages 80–3), and then remove the waste wood with a tenon saw and chisel.

MAKING A TEMPLATE

Cut a tapered plywood tongue, with one side angled for marking dovetails in softwood and the other for dovetailing hardwoods (see page 141). Glue the tongue into a slot cut in a hardwood stock.

▲ Marking the lap dovetail.

▲ Shaping the lap dovetail.

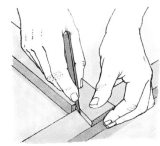

▲ Marking the recess.

Mortise and tenon joints

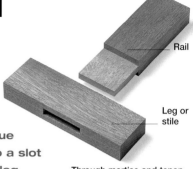

In the simplest version of this centuries-old, universally popular joint, the tenon (a tongue cut on the end of a rail) fits into a slot (the mortise) cut into a stile or leg.

Rail

Leg or stile

Through mortise and tenon

Through mortise and tenon

The through joint, where the tenon passes right through the leg, is used a great deal for constructional frames of all kinds.

Mark the position and length of the mortise, using the rail as a template. Square the lines all round with a pencil **(1)**. Set a mortise gauge to match the width of the mortise chisel to be used, and then scribe the mortise centrally between the squared lines on both edges **(2)**.

Mark the shoulders on the rail. Score the shoulder lines with a marking knife **(3)**. Without adjusting the settings, use the mortise gauge

▲ **1** Marking the length of the mortise.

▲ **2** Scribing the mortise.

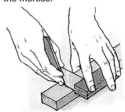

▲ **3** Marking the tenon shoulders.

▲ **4** Scribing the tenon.

MAKING JOINTS

138

to scribe the tenon on both edges and across the end of the rail **(4)**. Clamp the work to a bench so that you can stand at one end of the stile. Holding the chisel vertically, drive it 3 to 6mm (⅛ to ¼in) into the wood at the centre of the marked mortise **(5)**. Work backwards in short stages, making similar cuts.

Turn the mortise chisel around and chop the wood in stages towards the other end of the mortise. Lever out the waste with the chisel, then chop out another section of wood until you have cut halfway through the stile **(6)**. Pare the ends of the mortise square, then turn the work over, clamp the stile down again and chop out the waste from the other side of the joint **(7)**.

Clamp the rail in a vice, set at an angle so that the end grain faces away from you. Saw down to the shoulder on the waste side of each scribed line **(8)**. Turn the work around and do the same on the other side.

Clamp the work upright and saw parallel to the shoulder on both sides of the tenon, taking care not to overrun the marks **(9)**.

Holding the rail on a bench hook, remove the waste by sawing down the shoulder line on each side of the tenon **(10)**.

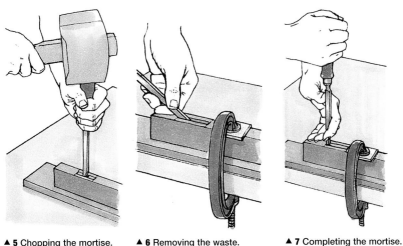

▲ **5** Chopping the mortise. ▲ **6** Removing the waste. ▲ **7** Completing the mortise.

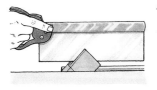

▲ **8** Sawing the tenon.

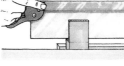

▲ **9** Cutting square.

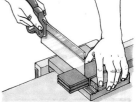

▲ **10** Sawing the shoulders.

Dovetail joints

**Traditional drawer-making
employs the inherent strength
of the dovetail joint, which
can resist the pressures of
opening and closing.**

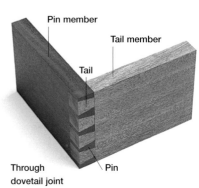
Through
dovetail joint

Through dovetail joint

The ability to cut tight-fitting dovetail joints seems to be regarded as the ultimate test of the woodworker's skill. It is also, undeniably, one of the most efficient joints for constructing boxes and cabinets from solid wood. Through dovetails, the most basic form of the joint, are visible on both sides of a corner.

Plane square the ends of both workpieces and, with a cutting gauge set to the thickness of the pin member, scribe the shoulder line for the tails on all sides of the other workpiece **(1)**.

A good hand-cut joint has equal-size tails matched with relatively narrow pins. Pencil a line across the end grain, 6mm (¼in) from each edge of the work, then divide the distance between the lines equally, depending on the required number of tails. Measure 3mm (⅛in) on each side of

these marks and square pencil lines across the end **(2)**.

Mark the sloping sides of each tail on the face side of the workpiece, using an adjustable bevel or a ready made dovetail template. Mark the waste with a pencil **(3)**.

Clamp it at an angle so that you can saw vertically beside each dovetail. When you have reached the last tail in the row, cant the work in the other direction and saw down the other side of each tail **(4)**.

▲ **1** Scribing the shoulder line.

▲ **2** Spacing the tails.

▲ **3** Marking out the tails.

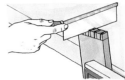
▲ **4** Cutting the tails.

Set the work vertically in the vice and remove the corner waste with the dovetail saw, then cut the waste from between the tails, this time using a coping saw **(5)**.

Use a bevel-edge chisel to trim what remains of the waste from between the tails. Finish flush with the shoulder line **(6)**.

Set the cutting gauge to the thickness of the tail member and scribe shoulder lines for the pins on the other component. Coat its end grain with chalk and clamp it upright. Position the cut tails precisely on the end of the workpiece, then mark their shape in the chalk with a pointed scriber or knife **(7)**.

Align a try square with the marks scored in the chalk, and draw parallel lines down to the shoulder on both sides of the work. Hatch the waste between the pins with a pencil **(8)**. Make fine saw cuts on both sides of

DOVETAIL ANGLES

The sides of a dovetail must slope at the optimum angle. An exaggerated slope results in weak short grain at the tips of the dovetail, while insufficient taper invariably leads to a slack joint.

Exaggerated slope

Insufficient taper

Ideally, mark a 1:8 angle for hardwoods, but increase the angle to 1:6 for softwoods. Tail proportion is a matter of choice, but a row of small, regularly spaced tails looks better than a few large ones, and also makes for a stronger joint.

each pin, following the angled lines marked across the chalked end grain **(9)**. Finish flush with the shoulder. Finally, trim the joint to a snug fit **(10)**.

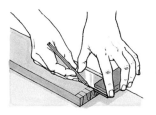
▲ **5** Removing the waste.

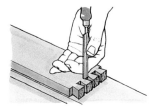
▲ **6** Trimming the shoulders.

▲ **7** Marking the pins.

▲ **8** Marking cutting lines.

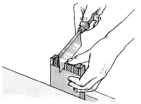
▲ **9** Cutting the pins.

▲ **10** Trimming the joint.

▶ Clamping joints for gluing

When gluing up any assembly, it pays to prepare the work area and rehearse the procedure in advance. This avoids delays that could lead to complications, especially when using a fast-setting adhesive.

Preparation

Assemble the parts without glue, to work out how many cramps you need and to allow you to adjust them to fit the work. You will find a helper most useful when clamping large or complicated assemblies.

It isn't necessary to glue every joint at once. For example, glue the legs and end rails of a table frame first; when these are set, glue the side rails between them.

Clamping a frame

The majority of frame and carcass joints need clamping in order to hold the assembly square until the adhesive sets. Prepare a pair of sash or pipe cramps, adjusting them so that the assembled frame fits between the jaws, allowing for softwood blocks to protect the work from the metal cramp heads. Carefully position the blocks to align with each joint – a misplaced or undersize block can distort the joint and bruise the wood.

1 Aligning the cramps

Apply adhesive evenly to both parts of each joint. Assemble the frame, ensuring that the cramps are

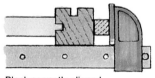

Block correctly aligned

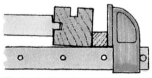

Block misaligned

▲ Carefully position softwood blocks to align with each joint.

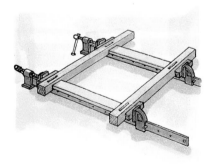

▲ Aligning the cramps.

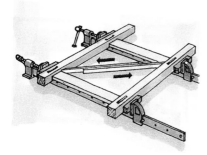

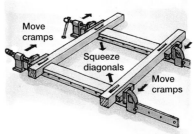

▲ Making pinch rods.

▲ Checking for square.

perfectly aligned with their respective rails, and gradually tighten the jaws to close the joints. Wipe off excess adhesive squeezed from the joints, using a damp cloth.

2 Making pinch rods

You can check the accuracy of a small frame with a try square at each corner, but for larger ones, measure the diagonals to ensure they are identical. Make a pair of pinch rods from thin strips of wood, planing a bevel on one end of each rod. Holding the rods back to back, slide them sideways until they fit diagonally across the frame, with a bevelled end tucked into each corner.

3 Checking for square

Holding the pinch rods together firmly, lift them out of the frame and check to see if they fit the other diagonal exactly. If the diagonals are different, slacken the cramps and set them at a slight angle to pull the frame square, then check the diagonals again.

WEB CRAMP

The web cramp applies equal pressure to the four corners of a mitred frame and can be used to clamp a stool or chair with turned legs – a difficult job with bar cramps.

A typical web cramp consists of a length of nylon webbing 25mm (1in) wide that is wound around a workpiece and pulled taut by a ratchet mechanism. The cramp is then tightened by turning the small ratchet nut with a spanner or screwdriver. After the glue has set, the tension is released by pressing the release lever.

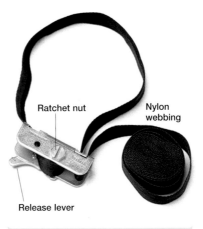

Ratchet nut

Nylon webbing

Release lever

▶ Knock-down fittings

Knock-down fittings – components or subassemblies joined
with mechanical fixings rather than adhesive – are designed
for use with square-cut butt joints. They are especially useful
when making large-scale constructions to be dismantled for
transportation and reassembly on site.

Block joints

This inexpensive,
surface-mounted
fitting consists of
interlocking plastic blocks screwed
on the inside of cabinet corners.

1 Fitting the socket blocks

Mark the thickness of the board on
the inside of the carcass side panel.
Mark the positions of two block
joints about 50mm (2in) from the
front and back edges. Align the
base of each socket block with the
marked lines, and screw it firmly
to the panel.

2 Fitting the dowel blocks

Holding the panels together at right
angles, fit the mating dowel blocks
and mark their fixing holes on the
other board. Screw the blocks in
place, and assemble the joint with
the clamping bolts.

Screw sockets

Threaded-metal screw
sockets provide
secure fixing points
for bolting together wood frames
or man-made boards.

1 Fitting a socket

Bore an 8mm (⅜in) diameter
stopped hole deep enough to set
the socket just below the surface of
the workpiece. Drive the fitting into
the hole, using a screwdriver in the
slot cut across the end of the
socket.

2 Assembling the components

Mark the centre of a clearance hole
for the bolt in the other component
and drill right through it, taking care
not to splinter the wood fibres on
the underside. Assemble the two
halves of the joint, clamping them
tightly with the bolt.

▲ Block joints: fitting
the socket blocks.

▲ Fitting the dowel
blocks.

▲ Screw sockets:
fitting a socket.

▲ Assembling the
components.

Bolt and barrel nut

This is a strong and positive fitting for all types of frame construction where the end of a rail meets the side of a leg or other vertical member. The bolt passes through a counterbored hole in the leg and into the end of the rail, where it is then screwed into a threaded barrel nut located in a stopped hole. A screw slot in the end of the nut allows you to align the threaded hole with the bolt.

1 Drilling the rail

Draw diagonals across the end of the rail to find the centre, and bore a clearance hole for the bolt where the lines cross. Calculate the distance from the end of the rail for the barrel nut, and drill a stopped hole in the side of the rail to intercept the bolt hole.

2 Drilling the leg

Mark and drill a counterbored clearance hole for the bolt and collar in the leg.

3 Fitting the locating dowel

Tap a panel pin into the end of the rail on its centre line, about 12mm (½in) from one edge. Crop the head off the pin, then assemble and tighten the fitting. Dismantle the joint, and drill a 6mm (¼in) stopped hole in the leg where the cropped pin left a mark. Remove the pin and drill the rail in the same way as the leg, then glue a short dowel in the hole.

Bolt and barrel nut fitting

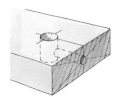

▲ Drilling the rail.

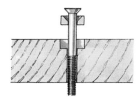

▲ Drilling the leg.

▲ Fitting the location dowel.

want to know more?

Take it to the next level...

Go to...
▶ **Planes** – pages 95–100
▶ **Woodworking cramps** – page 112
▶ **Sanding by hand** – pages 154–6

Other sources
▶ **Magazines**
   Good Woodworking
▶ **Second-hand woodworking books**
   search on Amazon (www.amazon.co.uk) or ebay (www.ebay.co.uk) for out-of-print books on woodworking or carpentry
▶ **Timber merchants**
   when purchasing wood, ask for advice if you are having problems with a project

finishing

wood

The versatility of natural wood means that some stunning finishes can be achieved, whatever it is that you choose to construct. These can be enhanced by any number of different polishes, stains and dyes that are widely available on the market today. Here we show you how to complete your project with style.

Filling cracks and holes

Although any woodworker rejects timber with major defects, it is unlikely that any batch of timber will be completely faultless and a few cracks and holes will need to be dealt with before sanding and finishing.

There are a number of materials and techniques to draw upon, depending on the dimensions of the crack or hole, and the type of finish planned.

Cellulose filler for paintwork

You can use a commercially prepared or home-made stopper when preparing wood for painting, or you can fill small holes and cracks with ordinary decorator's cellulose filler. Supplied ready-made in tubs or as a dry powder for mixing with water, cellulose filler is applied and sanded flush in the same manner as wood putty.

Stopper

Wax filling sticks

Electric
soldering
iron

Shellac
sticks

Flexible
filling knife

FINISHING WOOD

Wood putty or stopper

Traditional filler made from wood dust mixed with glue still has its uses, but most wood finishers prefer to employ commercially prepared wood putty, or stopper, sold as a thick paste in tubes or small cans, for filling indentations. Stoppers are made in a range of colours to resemble common wood species.

Most stoppers are one-part pastes, formulated for either interior or exterior woodwork. Once set, they can be planed, sanded and drilled along with the surrounding wood; they remain slightly flexible, to absorb any subsequent movement that may be caused by the timber shrinking and expanding.

Catalysed two-part stoppers, intended primarily for larger repairs, set even harder than the standard pastes.

Reconstituting stopper

To keep wood stopper in usable condition, replace the lid or screw cap as soon as you have taken enough for your requirements. If you find that stored water-based stopper has stiffened, try standing the tin in warm water or place the container on a radiator to make the filler pliable.

Using wood putty

Make sure the wood is clean and dry. Using a flexible filling knife, press putty into the indentations, leaving the filler slightly raised for sanding flush after it has set. Drag the knife across a crack to fill it, then smooth the putty by running the blade lengthways. Fill deep holes in stages, allowing the stopper to harden between applications.

Filling large holes

Plug deep knotholes with solid wood. When the glue has set, fill gaps around the patch with wood stopper.

Filled shoulder lines are almost always discernible, but you can make passable repairs to gappy joints that have visible end grain, using a home-made filler.

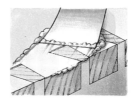

▲ Applying wood putty.

▲ Plug large knotholes with wood and finish with stopper.

FINISHING WOOD

149

▲ Colour-match putty with wood dye.

Colouring putty to match

To match the colour of your workpiece, make a test piece by applying stain and one finish coat to an offcut of the same wood. Select a putty that resembles the lightest background colour of the wood and, using a white ceramic tile as a palette, add compatible wood dye one drop at a time. Blend the dye into the putty with a filling knife to achieve the required tone.

Filling sticks

Sticks of solidified shellac in various colours are made for melting into holes in the wood or for building up broken mouldings. Shellac can be used as a preparatory stopper for use with most surface finishes.

Camauba wax, mixed with pigments and resins, is ideal for plugging small wormholes. Although wax filler can be applied to bare wood that is to be French-polished or waxed, it is often best to wait until the wood is finished.

Wax sticks are made in a range of colours. If necessary, cut pieces of wax from different sticks, blending them with the tip of a soldering iron to match a specific colour.

▲ Melt shellac with a soldering iron.

Filling with shellac

Use a heated knife blade or a soldering iron to melt the tip of a shellac stick, allowing it to drip into the hole. While it is still soft, press the shellac flat with a wood chisel dipped in water. As soon as the filler hardens, pare it flush with a sharp chisel, finishing with a fine abrasive.

Using wax filling sticks

Cut off a small piece of wax and put it on a radiator to soften. Using a pocket knife, press wax into the holes. As soon as it hardens, scrape the repair flush with an old credit card. Use sandpaper backing to burnish the wax filling.

▲ Burnish filling wax with the reverse side of a piece of sandpaper.

Abrasives

The surfaces of wood must be brought to as near perfect a finish as possible before beginning to apply varnish, lacquer or any other clear coating.

Rubbing wood smooth with abrasives is the usual way of getting the desired result, and woodworkers are today presented with an enormous range of products to achieve their aims.

Not only is the wood itself smoothed with abrasives, but each coat of finish is also rubbed

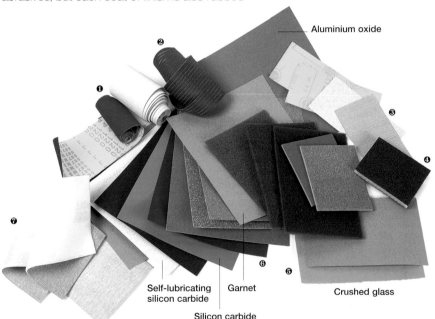

Aluminium oxide

Self-lubricating silicon carbide

Garnet

Crushed glass

Silicon carbide

▲ Abrasives

❶ Paper- or cloth-backed rolls
Economical and ideal for sanding turned legs and spindles.

❷ Slashed cloths
They can be crumpled in the hand and applied to work on the lathe.

❸ Velour-backed strips
Peel-off strips for sanding blocks and power sanders.

❹ Foam-backed pads
Flexible pads follow the contours of a workpiece.

❺ Non-woven pads
Nylon fibre impregnated with abrasive material.

❻ Standard-size sheets
Sandpaper or cloth sheets measure 280 x 230mm (11 x 9in).

❼ Flexible-foam pads
Ideal for sanding mouldings.

**Grading
sandpaper**
Sandpapers are
graded according to
particle size, and are
categorized as extra-
fine, fine, medium,
coarse or extra-
coarse. These
classifications are
adequate for most
purposes, but for
more precisely
graded abrasives,
each category is
divided by number –
the higher the
number, the finer
the grit.

over lightly, to remove specks of dust and other debris that become embedded as the finish sets.

Although sandpaper as such is no longer manufactured, the term is still used to describe all forms of abrasive, and we still 'sand' wood by hand and with power tools. Most abrasives are now manufactured using synthetic materials that are far superior to the sandpaper of old.

Abrasive materials

You can choose from a number of abrasive grits, depending on their relative costs and the nature of the material you are finishing.

Crushed glass is used to make inexpensive abrasive paper, intended primarily for sanding softwood that is to be painted.

Garnet is a natural mineral which, when crushed, produces relatively hard particles with sharp cutting edges. Reddish-brown garnet paper is used by cabinetmakers for sanding softwoods and hardwoods.

Aluminium oxide is used to manufacture a great many abrasive products for sanding by hand and with power tools.

Silicon carbide is the hardest and most expensive woodworking abrasive. It is an excellent material for sanding hardwoods, MDF and chipboard, but it is most often used for manufacturing abrasive paper and cloth for rubbing down between coats of varnish and paint.

Backing

The backing is basically nothing more than a vehicle that carries the grit to the work. Nevertheless, the choice of backing material can be crucial to the performance of the abrasive.

Paper is the cheapest backing material used in the manufacture of woodworking abrasives. It is

Abrasive   Size   Maker
grain   coat   coat   Backing

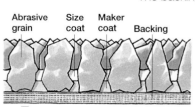

▲ Structure of an abrasive sheet.

available in a range of thicknesses or 'weights'.

Cloth or woven-textile backings provide very tough and durable, yet flexible, abrasive products.

Non-woven nylon-fibre pads, impregnated with aluminium-oxide or silicon-carbide grains, are ideal for rubbing down finishes and for applying wax polish and oil.

Foamed plastic is used as a secondary backing when you need to spread even pressure over a contoured surface.

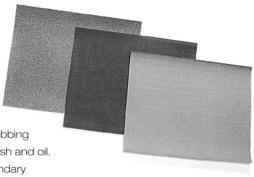

▲ Three different grades of sandpaper

Bond

The bond, or method of gluing abrasives to the backing, is vital, both in ensuring that the grit stays put, and because it affects the characteristics of sandpaper. Animal glue, which softens with heat generated by sanding, is used when flexibility is a requirement. Resin, on the other hand, is heat-resistant, making it ideal for power sanding. Because it is waterproof, resin is also used for the manufacture of wet-and-dry papers. A combination of adhesives modifies the properties of a paper. Resin over glue, for example, would make a relatively heat-resistant paper that would be more flexible than a resin-over-resin combination.

Additives

A third coating of stearate, a powdered soap, packs the spaces between the grains, presenting a finer abrasive surface to the work and reducing premature clogging with wood dust. Stearate, and other chemical additives, act as dry lubricants for abrasives used for rubbing down coats of hard finish.

Antistatic additives in the size coat reduce clogging dramatically and increase the efficiency of dust extractors. This leads to a decrease in dust deposits on the work.

MUST KNOW

Closed or open coat
Sandpapers can be categorized according to the density of grit. A closed-coat sandpaper is densely packed with abrasive grains and cuts relatively quickly. An open-coat sandpaper has larger spaces between the grains, which reduces clogging and is more suitable for resinous softwoods.

Sanding by hand

Most woodworkers use power sanding in the early stages of preparing a workpiece, but it is usually necessary to finish by hand, especially if the work includes mouldings. You can, of course, do the whole thing by hand – it just takes longer.

Always sand parallel to the grain, working from coarser to finer grits so that each application removes the scratches left by the previous paper or cloth. Stroking abrasives across the grain leaves scratches that are difficult to remove.

You will find it easier to sand most components before assembly, but take care not to round over the shoulders of a joint or create a slack fit by removing too much wood.

SANDING BLOCKS

It is much easier to sand a flat surface evenly if you wrap a piece of abrasive paper around a sanding block. Factory-made cork or rubber sanding blocks are very cheap and widely available.

Most blocks are designed to be wrapped with a piece of sandpaper torn from a standard sheet, but you can buy sanding blocks that take ready-cut self-adhesive or velour-backed strips of abrasive that are peeled off when they need replacing or pre-prepared sanding pads.

TEARING SANDPAPER

Fold a sheet of sandpaper over the edge of a bench, and tear it into strips that fit your sanding block. Wrap a piece of the paper around the sole of the block, gripping the sides with fingers and thumb.

Velcro-lined foam plastic Double-sided Cork Rubber

Sanding techniques

Sanding flat surfaces

Stand beside the bench so that you can rub a sanding block in straight strokes, parallel with the grain; sweeping your arm in an arc tends to leave cross-grain scratches. Work at a steady pace, letting the abrasive do the work. It pays to change the paper frequently, rather than tiring yourself by rubbing harder to achieve the same ends.

Cover the surface evenly, keeping the block flat on the wood at all times, especially as you approach the edges of the work, or you may inadvertently round over sharp corners.

Sanding end grain

Before sanding, stroke end grain with your fingers to determine the direction of fibre growth. It will feel smoother in one direction than the other; to achieve the best finish, sand in the smoothest direction.

MUST KNOW

Sanding sequence

Every woodworker develops his or her preferred sequence for preparing a workpiece for finishing, but the following will serve as a guide to suitable grades of abrasive to achieve the result.

Start with 120 grit aluminium-oxide or garnet paper followed by 180 grit, until the surface appears smooth and free from tool marks and similar blemishes. You only need to resort to anything as coarse as 80 to 100 grit if the wood is not already planed to a reasonably smooth surface.

Remove the dust between sandings, using a tack rag – a sticky cloth designed for picking up dust and fine debris. If you fail to keep the work clean, abrasive particles shed during the previous sanding may leave relatively deep scratches in the surface.

Sand again for no more than 30 to 60 seconds, using 220 grit, then raise the grain by wiping the surface with a damp cloth. Wait for 10 to 20 minutes, by which time the moisture will have caused the minute wood fibres to expand and stand proud of the surface. Lightly skim the surface with a fresh piece of 220 abrasive to remove these 'whiskers', leaving a perfectly smooth surface. It is particularly important to raise grain before applying water-based products.

If you feel the workpiece demands an extra-special finish, raise the grain once more and rub down very lightly, using 320 grit paper or an impregnated nylon-fibre pad.

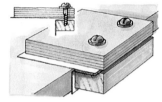

Sanding small items

It is impossible to clamp and sand small items using conventional methods. Instead, glue a sheet of sandpaper face-up on a flat board and rub the workpiece across the abrasive.

trapping two pieces of sandpaper face-to-face between them. Fold back one piece of paper to form a right angle. Rub the block along the edge of the work, simultaneously sanding both adjacent surfaces.

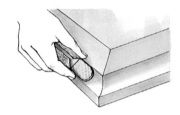

Sanding mouldings

Wrap sandpaper around a shaped block or dowel when sanding mouldings. Alternatively, use foam-backed paper or an impregnated nylon-fibre pad.

Sanding edges

It is even more difficult to retain sharp corners when sanding narrow edges. To keep the block level, clamp the work upright in a vice and, holding the block at each end, run your fingertips along each side of the work as you rub the abrasive back and forth. Finally, stroke the block lightly along the corner to remove the arris and prevent splinters.

Making an edge-sanding block

It is especially important to sand edges accurately when working on edge-veneered boards. Screw together two pieces of wood to make an edge-sanding block,

Checking a sanded surface

Inspect the workpiece against the light at a shallow angle, to check that the surface is sanded evenly and that you have removed all obvious scratches.

Power sanding

Nowadays, portable sanding machines relieve the woodworker from the tiresome chore of sanding for long periods. However, care must be taken not to inscribe scratches and whorls into the surface of the wood.

Belt sanders

These are heavy-duty power sanders that are capable of reducing even sawn timber to a smooth finish. As a result, they remove a great deal of wood very quickly, and have to be carefully controlled to avoid rounding over the edges of a workpiece or wearing through a layer of veneer.

▲ Belt sander

Using a belt sander

There are few occasions when you would need a belt sander for fine woodwork, but it is useful for smoothing large baulks of timber or some man-made boards. Switch on and gradually lower the sander onto the work. As soon as you make contact, move the sander forward – allowing the tool to remain stationary or dropping it heavily onto the surface will score the wood deeply. Sand in the direction of the grain only, keeping the tool moving and using parallel overlapping strokes. Lift the sander off the work before switching off.

Sanding belts

Cloth- and paper-backed belts are made for the average 60 to 100mm (2⅜ to 4in) wide sanders. They are held taut between two rollers, the front being adjustable to control tension and tracking. Operating a lever releases the tension so that you can change a belt. Once the sander is running, adjust a knob to centre the belt on the rollers.

▲ Using a belt sander.

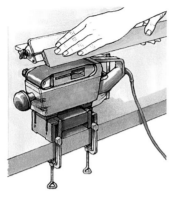

▲ Using a fixed belt sander.

Fixed belt sanders

Using a purpose-made cramp, you can attach a portable belt sander upside-down on a bench, allowing you to sand small components by applying them to the moving belt.

Orbital sanders

Provided you work through a series of progressively finer abrasives (see page 155) and raise the grain before the final light sanding, an orbital sander will produce a surface that, to all intents and purposes, is ready for finishing.

Palm-grip sanders

The majority of orbital sanders are designed to be held in both hands, but lightweight, palm-grip sanders are also available.

Sanding sheets

Strips of sandpaper are made specifically for use with orbital sanders. Designated as half, third and quarter sheets, their proportions are based

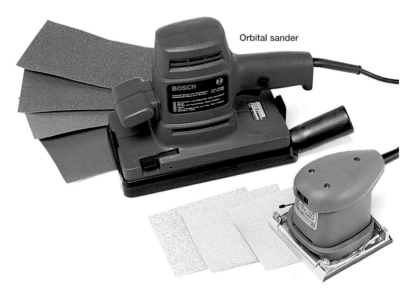

Orbital sander

Palm-grip sander

on the standard-size sheets made for hand-sanding. They are held in place by a wire clamp at each end of the sander's base plate; alternatively, strips are velourlined or self-adhesive for easy replacement. To preserve your health and reduce clogging, choose a sander that incorporates dust extraction,the base plate and sandpaper are both perforated so that dust is sucked directly from beneath the tool into a collecting bag or vacuum cleaner.

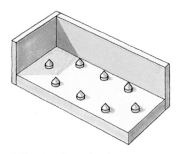

▲ Template for perforating ordinary sandpaper for an orbital sander.

Perforating sandpaper

Ready-made sheets are very convenient, but you can make considerable cost savings by perforating plain sandpaper strips or rolls. Using a soft pencil and white paper, make a rubbing of the perforations in your sander's base plate. Use it as a pattern for drilling matching holes in a piece of MDF, and glue into them short lengths of pointed dowel rod.

Attach a strip of abrasive to the base plate, and then press your sander down onto your perforator to pierce the sandpaper.

▲ Using an orbital sander.

Using orbital sanders

Don't apply excessive pressure to an orbital sander, as this tends to overheat the abrasive, causing dust and resin to clog the grit prematurely. A sensation of pins and needles in your fingers after prolonged sanding indicates that you are pressing too hard.

Keep the tool moving back and forth with the grain, covering the surface as evenly as possible.

Sanding into corners

With a well-designed orbital sander, it should be possible to sand into right angles and up to the ends of fixed rails or panels. However, for really tight corners and cross-grain mitres, use a delta sander, which has a triangular base plate.

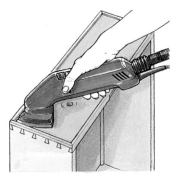

▲ A delta sander is useful for sanding into corners.

▲ Cordless sander

▲ Random-orbital sander

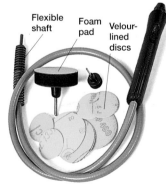

Flexible shaft   Foam pad   Velour-lined discs

▲ Flexible-shaft sander

Cordless sanders

There are obvious advantages to be gained from using a battery-powered sander: there's no electrical flex to get caught up on the workpiece, and you can work outside if you wish, completely independent of a mains supply.

Random-orbital sanders

The combined rotational and eccentric motions of a random-orbital sander practically eliminate discernible scratches on a wood surface. The circular base plate takes sanding discs, along with the usual options – a Velcro or self-adhesive attachment, and perforations for dust extraction. Some sanders can cope with flat and curved surfaces, while others have interchangeable base plates so that you can increase the sanding area for working on large boards or panels. The only disadvantage is that you cannot sand into corners.

Disc sanders

With the exception of bench-mounted machines, cabinetmakers seldom use disc sanders, which can score deep scratches in the wood. However, woodturners employ the combined actions of disc sander and lathe to their advantage for sanding bowls and platters.

Flexible-shaft sanders and discs

Arbor-mounted foam pads, from 25 to 75mm (1 to 3in) in diameter, are made for use in highly manoeuvrable, flexible-shaft sanders. Velour-lined or self-adhesive abrasive discs, with cloth or paper backing, come ready-made to fit every size of foam pad.

Advantages for woodturners

Miniature disc sanders are ideal for intricate woodwork such as carving or modelmaking, but they are especially suited to woodturners, because the soft-foam pads conform to the changing contours of a wooden bowl or vase.

Bench-mounted sanders

A relatively large-diameter metal disc sander, mounted rigidly to the bench, is perfect for finishing end grain. Using coarse to fine grits, you can also shape workpieces with a disc sander. Keep the workpiece moving, and press the end grain lightly against the downward-rotating side of the disc. Applying excessive pressure invariably scorches the wood.

▲ Bench-mounted disc sander

PROTECTING YOURSELF FROM DUST

Power sanders are not especially dangerous, provided they are used with care. However, the dust generated by sanding can be very injurious to health, and may also constitute a fire hazard.

Face masks and helmets

At the very least, make sure you wear a face mask to cover your nose and mouth when sanding. Cheap disposable masks are available from any tool store, and are usually supplied as part of the kit when you hire power sanders.

A battery-powered respirator, built into a lightweight helmet, offers the ultimate protection. A stream of filtered air, blown behind the transparent face screen, prevents you breathing airborne dust.

Dust extractors

Good-quality power sanders are fitted with an extractor port that discharges dust into a bag, for disposal after work or when the bag is full. For greater efficiency, attach a sander to an industrial vacuum cleaner that sucks the dust directly from the work surface. A purpose-made extractor is activated as you switch on the sander.

Scraping wood

Even though sanding is the most-used method for smoothing timber, scraping the surface, which removes minute shavings instead of dust particles, produces a superior finish.

Cabinet scrapers

The standard cabinet scraper is nothing more than a small rectangle of tempered steel. For shaped surfaces and mouldings, you need a scraper with a pair of curved edges.

Controlling a cabinet scraper

Holding the scraper in both hands, lean it away from you and push it forwards. Bending a scraper, by pressing your thumbs near the bottom edge, concentrates the forces in a narrow band, so that you can scrape small blemishes from the wood. Experiment with different curvatures and angles to vary the action and cutting depth.

Levelling wood panels

To scrape a panel flat and level, work in two directions at a slight angle to the general direction of grain. To finish, smooth the wood by scraping parallel with the grain.

▲ Controlling a cabinet scraper.

▲ Work in two directions at a slight angle to the grain.

PREPARING A SCRAPER

Before using a scraper, you must prepare and sharpen its cutting edges.

1 Filing a scraper
Clamp the scraper in a bench vice and draw-file its two long edges to make them perfectly square.

2 Honing the scraper
Filing leaves rough edges that must be rubbed down with an oiled slipstone.

3 Raising a burr
Stretch the metal along both cutting edges with a smooth metal burnisher. Strop each edge firmly four or five times.

4 Turning the burr
For the scraper to function, the raised burrs must be folded over at right angles.

Filling and sealing grain

An open-grain timber, such as oak or ash, looks good when coated with a satin varnish or oil, but when French polish or gloss varnish sinks into each pore, the result is a speckled, pitted surface that detracts from the quality of the finish.

To solve this problem, the majority of woodworkers opt for a ready-mixed grain filler.

Make sure the surface is completely clean and dustfree. Dip a pad of coarse burlap into the grain filler and rub it vigorously into the wood, using overlapping circular strokes.

Before the paste dries, wipe across the grain with clean burlap to remove excess filler from the surface. Use a pointed stick to remove any paste. Leave the grain filler to dry thoroughly overnight, then sand lightly in the direction of the grain, using 220 grit, self-lubricating siliconcarbide paper. Rub down mouldings or turned pieces with an abrasive nylonfibre pad.

Finish the job by applying sanding sealer. Sand well and pick up the dust with a tack rag. Brush sanding sealer onto the wood and leave to dry for a few hours. Rub the surface with fine sandpaper, an abrasive pad or 0000-grade steel wool before applying your chosen finish. You may need a second sealing coat on very porous timber.

▲ Applying grain filler.

▲ Removing excess filler.

▲ Rubbing down.

Bleaching wood

Woodworkers often resort to bleaching in order to obliterate staining. For this, you should use a comparatively mild bleach, such as a solution of oxalic acid. You can also use bleach to reduce the depth of colour of a workpiece.

To alter the colour of timbers drastically, you need a strong proprietary two-part bleach. This is usually sold in kit form, comprising a pair of clearly labelled plastic bottles, one containing an alkali and the other hydrogen peroxide. However, the bottles are invariably labelled A and B, or 1 and 2.

Because some woods bleach better than others, it is worth testing a sample before you treat the actual workpiece. As a rough guide, ash, beech, elm and sycamore are easy to bleach, whereas you may have to bleach other woods, such as mahogany, rosewood and oak a second time to get the colour you want.

Pour some of the contents of bottle A into a container and, using a nylon brush, wet the workpiece evenly.

About 5 to 10 minutes later, during which time the wood may darken, take another brush and apply the second solution. The chemical reaction causes foaming on the surface of the wood.

When it is dry, neutralize the bleach by washing the work with a weak acetic-acid solution, comprising one teaspoon of white vinegar in a pint of water. After about three days, sand down the raised grain and apply the finish.

WATCH OUT!

- Wood bleach is a dangerous substance which must be handled with care.
- Wear protective gloves, goggles and an apron.
- Wear a face mask when sanding wood that has been bleached.
- Ventilate the workshop.
- Rinse your skin immediately if you splash yourself with bleach. If you are going to work outside, fill a bucket with water.
- If you get bleach in your eyes, rinse well with running water and seek medical attention.

▲ Applying solution A.

▲ Applying solution B.

▲ Neutralizing the bleach.

Stains and dyes

A wood stain or dye is different from a surface finish such as paint in that a true penetrating dye or stain soaks deep into the wood. However, it provides no protection at all, and so a clear finish is always applied to a stained workpiece afterwards.

Modern stains often contain translucent pigments that lodge in the pores of the wood, accentuating the grain. Successive applications of a pigmented stain gradually darken the wood, whereas applying more than one coat of a non-pigmented stain has little effect on the colour.

Solvent or oil stains

The most widely available penetrating stains, made from oil-soluble dyes, are thinned with

❶ Solvent or oil stains
❷ Acrylic stains
❸ Methylated spirit
❹ Ready-mixed water stains
❺ White spirit
❻ Ready-mixed spirit stains
❼ Concentrated water stains
❽ Powdered water stains

white spirit. Known as solvent stains or oil stains, these wood dyes are easy to apply evenly, will not raise the grain and dry relatively quickly.

▲ Laminated beech barstool enhanced by the use of several coloured dyes.

Spirit stains

Traditional spirit stains are made by dissolving aniline dyes in methylated spirit. The main disadvantage with spirit stains is their extremely rapid drying time, which makes it difficult to get even coverage without leaving darker patches of overlapping colour.

Water stains

Water stains are available from specialists as readymade wood-colour dyes. You can also buy them as crystals or powders for dissolving in hot water so that you can mix any colour you want. Water stains dry slowly, which means there is plenty of time to achieve an even distribution of colour, but you must allow adequate time for the water to evaporate completely before you apply a finish. They also raise the grain, leaving a rough surface, so it is essential to wet the wood and sand down prior to applying water stains.

Acrylic stains

The latest generation of water stains, based on acrylic resins, are emulsions that leave a film of colour on the surface of the wood. They raise the grain less than traditional water stains and are more resistant to fading. As well as the usual wood-like colours, acrylic stains are made in a range of pastel shades; it can, however, be difficult to predict the final colour produced by these pastel-coloured stains on dark hardwoods.

MUST KNOW

Compatibility
You can create practically any colour you like by mixing compatible wood stains or dyes, and you can reduce the strength of a colour by adding more of the relevant solvent However, you should guard against overlaying a penetrating stain, even one that has dried out, with a surface finish that contains a similar solvent. As you drag a brush or pad across the surface, the solvent may reactivate the colour, causing it to 'bleed'into the surface finish.

As a basic rule, select a stain that will not react with the finish you want to apply, or seal the stain first to prevent solvent disturbing the colour. It is always worth testing the stain and finish before applying either to a workpiece.

Applying penetrating stains

Wet the surface to get some idea of what a particular workpiece will look like under a clear finish, and if in doubt, apply some of the actual finish you intend to use. If you are unhappy with the resultant depth of colour, or if you feel it doesn't quite match another piece of wood you are working with, take a scrap piece of the same timber and make a test strip to try out a stain before colouring the workpiece itself. This saves heartache later on!

▲ Equipment for applying stains and dyes: paintbrush, decorator's paint pad, soft cloth, PVC gloves.

MAKING A TEST STRIP

Before you colour an actual workpiece, make a test strip to see how the wood will be affected by the stain you intend to use. It is important that the test strip is sanded as smooth as the workpiece you will be staining, because coarsely sanded wood absorbs more dye and will therefore appear darker than the same piece of wood prepared with a finer sandpaper

Apply a coat of stain and allow it to dry. As a general rule, stains dry lighter than they appear when wet Apply a second coat to see if it darkens the wood, leaving part of the first application exposed for comparison. If you apply more than two full coats of stain, the colour may become patchy due to uneven absorption of the liquid.

A second coat of a non-pigmented stain may not change the colour appreciably, but you can modify it by overlaying with a compatible stain of a different colour.

Once the stain is completely dry, paint one half of the test strip with the intended finish to see how it affects the colour of the stain.

Test strip, using
non-pigmented
stain

Unfinished

Clear finish

Test strip, using
pigmented stain

Unfinished

Clear finish

Staining and dyeing techniques

Preparing a workpiece for staining

Sand the workpiece well (see pages 154–61), making sure that there are no scratches or defects that will absorb more stain than the surrounding wood. In addition, scrape off any patches of dried glue that could affect the absorption of stain.

Applicators

You can use good-quality paintbrushes, decorators' paint pads covered with mohair pile, non-abrasive polishing pads (see page 151), or a wad of soft cloth to apply penetrating stains. You can also spray wood dyes, provided you have adequate extraction facilities and good ventilation. Wear PVC gloves and old clothes or an apron when applying wood stains. You may also need a face mask.

Setting up for staining

Plan the work sequence in advance, to minimize the possibility of stain running onto adjacent surfaces or one area of colour drying before you can 'pick up' the wet edges. If you have to colour both sides of a workpiece, stain the least important side first, immediately wiping off any dye that runs over the edges.

STAINING SOFTWOOD

▲ Softwood coloured with penetrating stain (left) and varnish stain (right).

It is advisable to apply stain to softwood with a cloth pad rather than a paintbrush; highly absorbent wood tends to draw extra stain from a heavily loaded brush at the first point of contact, thus creating a patch of darker colour.

The different rates of absorption between earlywood and latewood often give stained softwood a distinctly striped appearance. With some colours, this can be very attractive, but if it doesn't suit your requirements, try colouring the wood with varnish stain or dark-coloured wax to alleviate the problem.

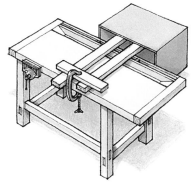

Staining large panels

If possible, set up the workpiece so that the surface to be stained is horizontal. Lay a large panel or door on a pair of trestles so that you can approach it from all sides.

Batch production

It is sometimes convenient to stain components before assembly, setting them aside to dry while you complete the batch.

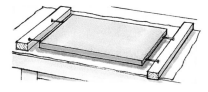

To colour a number of adjustable bookshelves, for example, drive a pair of nails or screws into each end. Lay each shelf on a bench, with the nails or screws resting on battens to raise the shelf off the work surface. Having stained each side in turn, stand the shelf on end against a wall until the stain is dry.

Supporting drawers and cabinets

After staining the inside of drawers or small cabinets, support them at a comfortable working height to complete the job, using cantilevered battens clamped or screwed temporarily to a bench.

Staining a flat surface

Pour enough stain to colour the entire workpiece into a shallow dish. Brush or swab the stain onto the wood in the direction of the grain, blending in the wet edges before the dye has time to dry. When you have covered the surface, take a clean cloth pad, and mop up excess stain, distributing it evenly across the workpiece. If you splash stain onto the wood, blend it in quickly to prevent a patchy appearance.

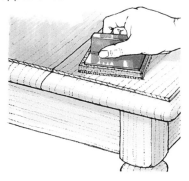

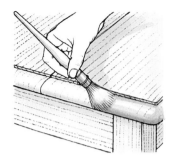

You can stain veneer patches or pieces of marquetry before gluing them in place. Dipping scraps of veneer in a dish of wood dye ensures even colouring.

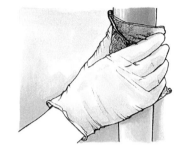

Staining end grain

Exposed end grain appears darker than the rest of the workpiece because the orientation of the cells allows it to absorb more penetrating stain. Painting the end grain with a coat of white shellac or sanding sealer will reduce the amount of colour taken up by the wood. Alternatively, you can use thinned varnish, but you should wait 24 hours before you stain the wood.

Staining turned spindles

Apply stain to turned legs and spindles with a rag or a non-woven polishing pad. Pub the dye well into turned beads and fluting, then cup the applicator around the leg or spindle and rub it lengthways.

Since turned work exposes end grain it is very difficult to obtain even coverage.

Colouring veneer

You can treat modern veneered panels like solid wood. However, old furniture was invariably veneered using water-soluble animal glue, and it would pay to use a spirit or solvent stain to colour such items.

Staining carved work

Use a soft brush to apply penetrating stain to carving or intricate mouldings, absorbing surplus stain immediately with rag or a paper towel.

Modifying the colour

No matter how practised you become at judging colours and mixing dyes, inevitably there comes a time when the dried stain is not quite the colour you had in mind. If it's too dark, you may be able to remove some stain, but don't make the mistake of trying to alter the colour by applying layer upon layer of dye – this will simply lead to muddy colours or poor finish adhesion. Instead, add washes of tinted finish to modify the colour gradually. This can be done by applying a coat of tinted shellac, a thinned wash of tinted varnish stain or a dressing of coloured wax.

▲ One way to modify the colour of a stained piece is to apply a tinted varnish.

If a solvent-stained workpiece dries streaky or too dark in tone, wet the surface with white spirit and rub it with an abrasive nylon pad. Wipe the surface with a cloth to lift some of the stain and redistribute the remainder more evenly.

ACCENTUATING MOULDINGS AND CARVING

You can bring a workpiece to life by using colour to add depth to carving and intricate mouldings. The process imitates the effects of natural wear, adding considerably to the appeal of antique or reproduction furniture and picture frames.

Highlighting
The simplest method is to wipe colour from the high points while the stain is wet. Alternatively, sand these areas lightly with an abrasive pad after the stain has dried, and wash off the dust, using a cloth dampened with solvent.

Shading
You can add depth to the most delicate of raised patterns, using dark stain mixed into diluted French polish. Seal the stained surface, then paint tinted shellac liberally onto carved and moulded areas of the workpiece, allowing it to flow into all the nooks and crannies. Wipe the colour off high points immediately, using a soft cloth, and allow the shellac to dry before applying a clear finish.

Varnishes and lacquers

At one time, the terms 'lacquer' and 'varnish' were used to describe specific finishes. Lacquer was for the most part a quick-drying clear coating, whereas a conventional varnish was a mixture of resins, oil and solvent that dried more slowly.

Nowadays, a great many finishes are so complex that they no longer fit exactly into either category, but manufacturers have continued to use the familiar terms so as not to disorientate their customers. As a consequence, the labels 'lacquer' and 'varnish' have become interchangeable; to avoid further confusion, the terms used here are those that you are most likely to encounter when buying wood finishes.

The bulk of varnishes and lacquers are clear to amber-coloured finishes, designed primarily to protect the wood and accentuate its natural grain pattern. There are also modified finishes that contain coloured dyes or pigments.

▼ Clear polyurethane varnish is a tough and attractive finish for all interior wood surfaces.

Applying varnish

There are no special skills to master when applying solvent-based or acrylic varnishes. However, a few basic procedures can help avoid some of the less obvious pitfalls.

Varnishing a flat panel

Supporting a large panel horizontally on a pair of trestles makes varnishing marginally easier, but there are few problems with finishing a hinged door or fixed panel, provided you guard against the varnish running.

1 Applying a sealer coat of oil varnish

Thin oil varnish by about 10 per cent when applying a first sealer coat to bare wood. You can brush it onto the wood, but some woodworkers prefer to rub it into the grain with a soft cloth.

2 Rubbing down the first coat

Leave the sealer coat to harden overnight, then hold the work in a good source of light to inspect the varnished surface. Rub it down lightly in the direction of the grain, using fine wet-and-dry paper dipped in water. Wipe the surface clean, using a cloth moistened with white spirit, and dry it with a paper towel.

3 Brushing full-strength varnish

Paint oil varnish onto the wood, brushing first with the grain then across it to spread the finish evenly. Always brush towards the area you have just finished, to blend the wet edges. It pays to work at a fairly brisk pace,varnish begins to set after about 10 minutes, and rebrushing it tends to leave permanent brushmarks. Finally 'lay

off' along the grain with very light strokes, using just the tips of the bristles to leave a smoothly varnished surface. When varnishing vertical surfaces, lay off with upward strokes of the brush.

Two full-strength coats of oil varnish should be sufficient. For a perfect finish, rub down lightly between each hardened coat.

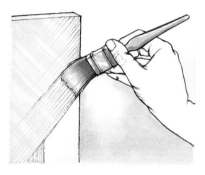

to run down the surface. To prevent this happening only brush along the moulding.

When finishing a panelled door, varnish the mouldings first and then varnish the panel, brushing out from each corner towards the centre.

Varnishing edges

As you approach the edges of a panel, brush outwards away from the centre. If you flex the bristles back against the sharp arris, you will cause varnish to dribble down the edge.

It is best to blend in the edges of a workpiece as the work progresses, but if that proves troublesome, try varnishing the edges of a panel first and letting them dry. When you coat the flat surfaces, wipe runs from the edges with a rag.

Varnishing mouldings

Flexing a brush across a moulding usually causes a teardrop of varnish

Matting a gloss varnish

Matt and satin oil varnishes have very finely textured surfaces that serve to scatter the light. These look perfect, but you can achieve

a smoother-feeling surface on components such as wooden chair arms or a table top by rubbing down a gloss varnish to a matt finish.

Rub the varnish with 000-grade steel wool dipped in wax polish. Leave the wax to harden, then burnish it with a soft duster to create the final finish.

APPLYING ACRYLIC VARNISH

Many of the techniques employed when applying oil varnish are just as relevant to the application of acrylic varnish. The aim is still to acquire a flat, even coating without runs or brushmarks, but the chemical properties of acrylic varnish make it behave slightly differently from oil varnish.

Grain-raising characteristics

When a piece of wood absorbs water, its fibres swell and stand up proud of the surface. Because it is waterbased, acrylic varnish has the same effect, making the final finish less than perfect. The solution is either to wet the wood first, and sand it smooth before applying acrylic varnish, or to sand the first coat of varnish with fine wet-and-dry paper dipped in water before re-coating the work (see pages 154–6). Wipe up the dust with a cloth dampened with water; a tack rag may leave oily deposits that will spoil the next coat of acrylic varnish.

Problems with rust

Applying any water-based finish over unprotected steel or iron fittings, including woodscrews and nails, will cause them to rust. Either remove metal fittings before you varnish the work, or protect them with a coat of dewaxed transparent shellac.

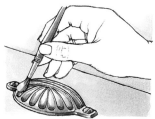

Don't use steel wool to rub down acrylic varnish; tiny slivers of metal that get caught in the grain may rust, creating black spots on the wood. Use copper wool or an abrasive nylon-fibre pad (see page 151).

Applying the varnish

Acrylic varnish must be applied liberally, first by brushing across the grain, then laying off evenly as described for applying oil varnish.

Acrylic varnish dries in only 20 to 30 minutes, so you need to work fast, especially on a hot day, to avoid leaving permanent brushmarks in the finish.

You can apply a second coat after two hours. A total of three coats is sufficient for maximum protection.

Applying cold-cure lacquer

This is a very different finish from conventional varnish. Although cold-cure lacquer is no more difficult to apply, it is important to be aware of how the curing process can be affected by inadequate preparation and inappropriate procedures.

Mixing cold-cure lacquer

Mix recommended amounts of hardener and lacquer in a glass jar or polythene container. Metal containers and other plastics may react with the hardener, preventing the lacquer from curing.

Once mixed, some cold-cure acquers are usable for about three days. However, you can extend the pot life to about a week by covering the jar with polythene, held in place with an elastic band. This type of lacquer will last even longer if you keep the sealed container, clearly marked, in a refrigerator.

Brush care

Once polymerization is complete, cold-cure lacquer becomes insoluble, so wash brushes in special lacquer thinner as soon as the work is complete.

Preparing the surface

As with any wood finish, the work must be smooth and clean; remove every trace of wax, which might prevent the lacquer curing.

Applying cold-cure lacquer

Adequate ventilation is important, especially when you are lacquering a floor. Brush on lacquer liberally, using a flowing action and blending in wet edges as you go. The lacquer will be touch dry in about 15 minutes; apply a second coat after an hour.

There is no need to rub down between coats, except to correct blemishes. It you use stearated abrasives, wipe the sanded surface with special lacquer thinner.

Modifying the finish

For a gloss finish, when the last coat is hard, sand smooth with wet and dry paper and water until it becomes matt. Using a burnishing cream on a damp cloth, buff to a high gloss, then rub with a duster. For satin, rub with 000-grade steel wool lubricated with wax polish.

Wax polishes

Making wax polish from basic ingredients is sometimes advocated by traditionalists, but since there is such a variety of excellent polishes readily available, there seems little point in introducing a complication into what is otherwise one of the simplest of wood-finishing processes.

Most commercially prepared wax polishes are a blend of relatively soft beeswax and hard carnauba wax, reduced to a usable consistency with turpentine or white spirit.

Paste wax polish

The most familiar form of wax polish is sold as a thick paste, packed in flat tins or foil containers. Paste wax, applied with a cloth pad or fine steel wool, serves as an ideal dressing over another finish.

Liquid wax polish

When you want to wax a large area of oak panelling, for example, it is probably easiest to brush on liquid wax polish that has the consistency of cream.

Floor wax

Floor wax is a liquid polish formulated for hardwearing surfaces. It is usually available as a clear polish only.

Woodturning sticks

Carnauba wax is the main ingredient for sticks that are hard enough to be used as a friction polish on workpieces being turned in a lathe.

▲ A traditional wax finish gives a sympathetic patina to a Georgian-style dressing table and chair.

▲ Tinted brushing polish deepens the colour of pine furniture.

▼ Wax-dressed walnut display cabinet.

Coloured polishes

White to pale-yellow polishes do not alter the colour of the wood to a great extent, but there is also an extensive choice of darker shades, sometimes referred to as staining waxes, that can be used to modify the colour of a workpiece and to hide scratches and minor blemishes. Dark-brown to black polish is a popular finish for oak furniture; it enhances the patina of old wood and, by lodging in the open pores, accentuates the grain pattern. There are warm golden-brown polishes, made to put the colour back into stripped pine, and orange-red polishes to enrich faded mahogany. Applying one polish over another creates even more subtle shades and tints.

It is not a good idea to wax chairs or benches with dark-coloured polishes in case your body heat should soften the wax and stain your clothing. The same goes for finishing the insides of drawers; long-term contact could discolour delicate fabrics.

Silicones

Silicone oil, which is added to some polishes to make them easier to apply and burnish, will repel most surface coatings should the piece require refinishing in the future. Sealing the wood beforehand is a wise precaution, but applying a chemical stripper at a later date may still allow silicone oil to penetrate the pores. You should therefore decide from the beginning whether it would be better to finish a piece with a silicone-free wax polish.

Applying wax polishes

Finishing wood with a wax polish could hardly be simpler, as it requires only careful application and sufficient energy to burnish the surface to a deep shine. However, as with any wood finish, the workpiece must be sanded smooth and any blemishes filled or repaired before you can achieve a satisfactory result. Wipe the surface with white spirit to remove traces of grease and old wax polish.

Although there is no need to fill the grain, it is always best to seal the work with two coats of French polish or sanding sealer before applying wax polish, especially if you have coloured the wood with solvent stain. Rub down the sealer coats with fine silicon-carbide paper.

▲ Applying paste wax polish.

▲ Rubbing on more polish with steel wool.

Paste wax polish

Dip a cloth pad in paste wax and apply the first coat, using overlapping circular strokes to rub the wax into the grain. Cover the surface evenly, then finish by rubbing in the direction of the grain. If the polish proves difficult to spread, warm the tin on a radiator.

After about 15 to 20 minutes, use 000-grade steel wool or an abrasive nylon pad to rub on more wax polish, this time working along the grain. Put the work aside for

WAX-POLISHING BRUSHES

Professional wood finishers sometimes use a bristle brush to burnish hardened wax polish. You can use a clean shoe brush, but you might want to buy a purpose-made furniture brush fitted with a handle to keep your knuckles out of the way when burnishing into awkward corners and recesses. In addition, there are circular brushes designed to fit the chuck of a power drill; when you are using one of these, apply light pressure only and keep the brush moving across the polished surface.

Drill brush

Hand brush for wax polish

Shoe brush

Furniture brush

24 hours so that the solvent can evaporate. On new work, apply four or five coats of wax in all, allowing each one to harden overnight.

When the wax has hardened thoroughly, burnish vigorously with a soft cloth pad. Some polishers prefer to use a furniture brush because it raises a better shine, particularly when burnishing carved work. Finally, rub over all polished surfaces with a clean duster.

▲ Pour some wax polish into a small dish and brush liberally onto the surface.

Liquid wax polish

Decant some polish into a shallow dish and brush it liberally onto the wood, spreading the wax as evenly as possible. Let the solvent evaporate for about an hour.

Apply a second coat of wax with a soft cloth pad. Use circular strokes at first, and finish by rubbing parallel to the grain. An hour later, apply a third coat if required.

Leave the polish to harden, preferably overnight, then burnish the workpiece in the direction of the grain with a clean soft duster.

Maintaining a wax finish

The colour and patina of a wax finish improve with age, provided the finish receives regular care. Mop up any spilled water immediately, and dust a polished surface frequently to pick up dirt that might otherwise sink into the wax and discolour the finish. If you cannot raise a satisfactory shine by burnishing with a soft cloth, it is time to apply a fresh coat of wax. Very dowdy wax polish can be removed with white spirit, in preparation for refinishing.

APPLYING A WAX DRESSING

If you want to achieve the typical mellow finish of wax polish but prefer something more hardwearing, you can apply a thin wax dressing over polyurethane varnish or cold-cure lacquer.

Dip 000-grade steel wool or an abrasive nylon pad in paste polish, and rub the finished surface using long straight strokes, parallel with the grain. Leave the wax to harden for 15 to 20 minutes, then polish it with a soft cloth.

Oil finishes

Some woodworkers consider oil finishes as being suitable only for hardwoods such as teak or afrormosia. However, oil makes a handsome finish for any timber, especially pine, which turns a rich golden colour when oiled.

Linseed oil, derived from the flax plant, is rarely used nowadays for finishing wood, mainly because it can take up to three days to dry. Manufacturers have been able to reduce this to about 24 hours by heating the oil and adding driers, producing 'boiled' linseed oil. Neither type of oil should be used as an exterior finish.

Tung oil, also known as Chinese wood oil, is obtained from nuts grown in China and parts of South America. A tung-oil finish is resistant to water, alcohol and acidic fruit juice, takes about 24 hours to dry and is suitable for exterior woodwork. Commercial wood-finishing oils, based on tung oil, include synthetic resins to improve their durability.

Pure tung oil is non-toxic, but some manufacturers add metallic driers to it, so don't use tung oil for items that will come into contact with food unless the maker's recommendations state specifically that it is safe to do so. As an alternative, use ordinary olive oil or one of the special 'salad-bowl' oils, sold for finishing food receptacles and chopping boards.

Gelled oil is a blend of natural oils and synthetic resin in a thick gel. It behaves more like a soft wax polish and can be applied to bare wood as well as over existing finishes such as varnish and lacquer.

▲ Pine staircase finished with hardwearing gelled oil.

Oil-finishing techniques

Preparing the surface

Since oil is a penetrating finish, it cannot be applied to a pre-varnished or painted workpiece; strip a surface finish using chemical stripper. When finishing previously oiled timber, use white spirit to clean old wax from the surface. Prepare bare wood thoroughly.

2 Applying additional oil with a pad

After six hours, use an abrasive nylon-fibre pad to rub oil onto the wood in the general direction of the grain. Wipe excess from the surface with a paper towel or cloth pad, then leave it to dry overnight. Apply a third coat in the same way.

1 Oiling bare wood

Shake the container before decanting some oil into a shallow dish. Apply the first coat, using a fairly wide paintbrush to wet the surface thoroughly. Leave the oil to soak in for about 10 to 15 minutes, then ensure that coverage is even by wiping excess oil from the surface with a soft cloth pad.

3 Modifying the finish

Leave the last coat to dry thoroughly, then burnish the surface with a duster to raise a soft sheen.

For a smooth satin finish, dress interior woodwork with wax polish, using a clean abrasive nylon pad or fine steel wool.

Oiling turned pieces

After sanding a turned workpiece, switch off the lathe while you rub oil onto the wood. Let it soak in for a short while, wipe off excess oil, then restart the lathe and burnish

> **WATCH OUT!**
>
> ### Fire precautions
> As oil oxidizes it generates heat, which can cause oil-soaked rags to burst into flames. Spread out used rags to dry thoroughly outside, or soak them in a bucket of water overnight before disposing of them.

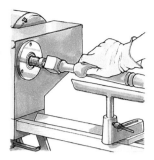 

by holding a cloth pad against the slowly rotating workpiece.

Applying gelled oil

Apply gelled oil to bare wood, using a soft cloth pad to rub the finish vigorously in the direction of the grain until the surface is touch-dry. Two coats are usually sufficient, but apply more gelled oil to a workpiece that will be subjected to heavy wear and hot dishes, allow four hours between coats. Apply gelled oil sparingly over an existing finish.

Since gelled oil dries naturally to a soft sheen, there is no need to burnish the workpiece again.

MUST KNOW

Faults and remedies

Oiling wood is so easy that success is practically guaranteed, provided you have prepared the workpiece adequately and you don't leave the oil to become sticky.

Sticky surface

If you leave excess oil on the surface for longer than about an hour, it thickens and becomes sticky. Don't attempt to wipe off oil if it reaches this stage. Instead, use an abrasive nylon pad to apply a light dressing of fresh oil to wet the surface again, then wipe over with a cloth pad or absorbent paper towel.

White rings

Hotplates or dishes may leave white rings on an oiled surface. These blemishes are usually temporary and disappear of their own accord within a short time.

want to know more?

Take it to the next level...

Go to...
▶ **The colour of wood** – page 25
▶ **Softwoods of the world** – pages 28–39
▶ **Hardwoods of the world** – pages 40–66

Other sources
▶ **Books**
the more advanced can try *The Fine Art of Cabinet Making* by James Krenov; *Furniture Restoration – A Manual of Techniques* by Graham Ushe
▶ **Training courses**
further your woodworking skills by following a course that awards an NVQ qualification at the end of it. Contact your local college or go online

---

Glossary

Air drying Method for seasoning timber that permits covered stacks of sawn wood to dry naturally in the open air.

Arc Part of an unbroken curved line as drawn by a compass.

Arris The sharp edge where two surfaces meet at an angle.

Axis Imaginary line about which an object such as a chair rail is symmetrical.

Backing grade Category of cheaper veneers that are glued to the back of a board in order to balance better-quality veneers glued to the front face.

Banding Plain or patterned strip of veneer used to make decorative borders.

Batten Strip of wood.

Bead A rounded convex shape turned on a lathe. *or* A fine moulded strip of wood, also known as beading.

Bevel A surface that meets another at an angle other than a right angle.

Biscuit Small oval plate of compressed wood that fits into a slot cut in both halves of a joint as a means of reinforcement.

Blank Piece of wood roughly cut to size ready for turning on a lathe.

Blockboard Man-made building board with a core of approximately square-section solid-wood strips sandwiched between thin plywood sheets. *See also* laminboard.

Bond Method of gluing the abrasive to the paper or cloth backing of materials used for smoothing wood.

Bore To drill a hole.

Bowing Lengthwise bending of a piece of wood as a result of shrinkage.

Bruise To dent timber by striking it with a hard object such as a hammer.

Burr Warty growth on the trunk of a tree; when sliced, it produces speckled burr veneer. *or* An extremely thin strip of metal left along the cutting edge of a blade after honing or grinding.

Buttress Roughly triangular outgrowth at the foot of a tree trunk. Buttresses provide the tree with increased stability.

Calibrated Marked out with one or more scales of measurement.

Case-hardened Term used to describe unevenly seasoned timber with a moisture content that varies throughout its thickness.

Catalyst A substance that stimulates or increases the rate of a chemical reaction.

Cauls Sheets of wood or metal used to press veneer onto groundwork.

Chamfer A 45-degree bevel along the edge of a piece of wood, board or panel. *or* To cut such a bevel.

Chattering Noise caused by a workpiece vibrating.

Checks Splits in timber caused by uneven seasoning.

Chipboard Man-made building board composed of compressed particles of wood and glue.

Claw Split hammer peen used to grip a nail by its head and lever it out of a piece of wood or board.

Clear timber Good-quality wood, free from defects.

Closed-coat Term used to describe sandpaper that has abrasive particles packed closely together.

Coarse-textured See open grain.

Collet Tapered sleeve, made in two or more segments, that grips the shaft of a cutter or drill bit.

Comb-grain Another term for quarter-sawn.

Compound mitre A mitre angled in two planes.

Core The central layer of plies, particles or strips of wood in a man-made board.

Counterbore To cut a hole that

permits the head of a bolt or screw to lie below the surface of a piece of wood. *or* The hole itself.

Cove A concave moulding along the edge of a workpiece. *or* Another term for hollow.

Crest rail The top rail of the back rest of a chair.

Cross-banding Strips of veneer cut across the grain and used as decorative borders.

Crosscutting Sawing across the grain.

Cross grain Grain that deviates from the main axis of a workpiece or tree.

Crown-cut Term used to describe veneer that has been tangentially sliced from a log, producing oval or curved grain patterns.

Cupping The bending of a piece of wood across its width as a result of shrinkage.

Cure To set by means of a chemical reaction.

Curl figure The grain pattern of wood cut from the fork where a branch joins the trunk of a tree.

Curly figure *See* curly grain.

Curly grain Wood grain exhibiting an irregular wavy pattern.

Defect An abnormality or irregularity that decreases wood's working properties and value.

Dimension stock Prepared timber cut to standard sizes.

Double insulation A power tool with a non-conductive plastic casing that protects the user from electric shock is described as 'double-insulated'.

Draw-filing Smoothing metal by drawing a file across it with the teeth at a shallow angle to the surface being smoothed.

Dressed stock Another term for dimension stock.

Earlywood The part of a tree's annual growth rings that is laid down in the early part of the growing season.

Edge-grain Another term for quarter-sawn.

End grain The surface of wood exposed after cutting across the fibres.

Face edge The surface planed square to the face side, from which other dimensions and angles may be measured.

Face-quality veneer Better-quality veneer, used to cover the visible surfaces of a workpiece.

Face side The flat planed surface from which all other dimensions and angles are measured.

Feed To push a workpiece in a controlled manner towards a moving blade or cutter.

Fence Adjustable guide that keeps the cutting edge of a tool at a set distance from the edge of a workpiece.

Fibreboards Range of building boards made from reconstituted wood fibres.

Figure Another term for grain pattern.

Flat-grain Another term for plain-sawn.

Flat-sliced Term describing a narrow sheet of veneer that has been cut from part of a log with a knife.

Flat-sawn Another term for plain-sawn.

Flute Rounded concave groove.

Gauging Marking out a piece of wood with a marking gauge, mortise gauge or cutting gauge.

Grain The general direction or arrangement of the fibrous materials of wood.

Green wood Newly cut timber that has not been seasoned.

Groove Long narrow channel cut in the direction of the grain. *or* To cut such a channel.

Hardwood Wood cut from broadleaved trees that belong to the botanical group Angiospermae.

Heartwood The mature wood that forms the spine of a tree.

Hollows Concave shapes turned on a lathe.

Hone To produce the final cutting edge on a blade or cutter by rubbing it on or with an abrasive stone.
Housing Groove cut across the grain.

Inlay To insert pieces of wood or metal into prepared recesses so that the material lies flush with the surrounding surfaces.
Interlocked grain Bands of annual-growth rings with alternating right-hand and left-hand spiral grain.

Jig Device used to hold a workpiece or tool so that an operation can be repeated accurately.
Joiner Woodworker who specializes in the construction of building components such as windows, doors and stairs.

Kerf The slot cut by a saw.
Kiln drying A method for seasoning timber using a mixture of hot air and steam.
Knock-down fittings Mechanical devices for joining components, especially those that may have to be dismantled at a future date.
Knotting Shellac-based sealer used to coat resinous knots that would stain subsequent finishes.

Laminate A component made from thin strips of wood glued together. *or* To glue strips together to form a component.
Laminboard Man-made building board with a core of narrow strips of wood glued together and sandwiched between thin plywood sheets. *See also* blockboard.
Latewood The part of a tree's annual growth ring that is laid down in the later part of the growing season.
Lath Narrow strip of wood.
Long grain Grain that is aligned with the main axis of a workpiece. *See also* short grain.

Marquetry The process of laying pieces of veneer to make decorative patterns or pictures. *See also* parquetry.
Mitre Joint formed between two pieces of wood by cutting bevels at the same angle (usually 45 degrees) at the end of both pieces. *or* To cut such a joint.
Mortise A recess cut in timber to receive a matching tongue or tenon.
Muntin The central vertical member of a frame-and-panel door.

Nominal dimensions Standardized widths and thicknesses of timber newly sawn from a log.

Offcut Waste wood cut from a workpiece.
Open-grain timber Ring-porous wood with large pores. Also known as coarse-textured timber.
Outfeed The part of a machine's worktable behind the blade or cutter.
Oxidize To form a layer of metal oxide, as in rusting.

Pare To remove fine shavings with a chisel.
Parquetry Process similar to marquetry but using veneers cut into geometric shapes to make decorative patterns.
Particle boards Building boards made from small chips or flakes of wood bonded together with glue under pressure.
Patina The colour and texture that a material such as wood or metal acquires as a result of natural ageing.
Pilot hole Small-diameter hole drilled prior to the insertion of a woodscrew to act as a guide for the thread.
Plain-sawn Term used to describe a piece of wood with growth rings that meet the faces of the board at angles of less than 45 degrees.
Planed all round (PAR) Commercially prepared timber that has been planed smooth on both sides and both edges.
Plywood Board made by bonding a number of wood veneers together under pressure.

Quarter-sawn Term used to describe a piece of wood with growth rings at not less than 45 degrees to the faces of the board.

Rabbet Another term for rebate.
Rack To distort a frame or carcass by applying sideways pressure.
Ratchet Device that permits motion in one direction only.
Rebate Stepped recess along the edge of a workpiece, usually forming part of a joint. *or* To cut such a recess.
Ripsawing Cutting parallel to the grain.
Rubber Padded cloth used to apply polish, stain or varnish.

Sandpaper Generic term for abrasive papers used for smoothing wood.
Sapwood The new wood surrounding the denser heartwood.
Scribe To mark with a pointed tool. *or* To mark and shape the edge of a workpiece so that it will fit exactly against another surface, such as a wall or ceiling.
Season To reduce the moisture content of timber.
Section Drawing giving a view of a workpiece as if cut through.
Setting in Fine shaping of carved work.
Shellac Secretion of the lac insect used to manufacture French polish.
Shoot To plane accurately using a finely set plane.
Short grain Grain pattern where the general direction of the fibres lies across a narrow section of wood.
Side elevation Scale drawing showing the side view of a workpiece.
Softwood Wood cut from coniferous trees that belong to the botanical group Gymnospermae.
Spigot Short cylindrical projection on one component, designed to fit into a hole in another.
Spindle A length of wood that has been turned, such as a chair leg or a baluster.
Splitting out The breaking out of a cutter or drill bit through the bottom or back of a workpiece.
Stile A vertical side member of a frame-and-panel door.
Stop Strip of wood against which a door or a drawer front comes to rest when closed.
Straight grain Grain that aligns with the main axis of a tree or piece of wood.
Strop To sharpen a cutting edge until it is razor-sharp by rubbing it on a strip of leather. *or* The strip of leather itself.

Tang The pointed end of a chisel or file that is driven into the handle.
Template Cut-out pattern used to help shape a workpiece accurately.
Tenon Projecting tongue, on the end of a piece of wood, that fits into a corresponding mortise.
Thinner Substance used to reduce the consistency of paint, varnish or polish.
Tongue Projecting ridge, cut along the edge of a board, that fits into a corresponding groove in another board.

Veneer A thin slice of wood used as a surface covering – usually on a less expensive material such as a man-made board.
Vertical grain Another term for quarter-sawn.

Waney edge The natural wavy edge of a plank (sometimes still covered with tree bark).
Wavy grain The even wave-like grain pattern of wood that has an undulating cell structure.
Wild grain Irregular grain that changes direction, making the wood difficult to work.
Winding A warped or twisted board is sometimes said to be 'winding'

Yacht varnish An exterior-grade varnish especially suitable for coastal climates.

Need to know more?

Bibliography

Abbott, Mike, *Green Woodwork: Working with Wood the Natural Way* (Guild of Master Craftsmen, 1999)

Bowler, John, *Basic Woodwork (Mini Workbook S.)* (Murdoch Books UK, 1998)

Bowler, John, *Basic Carpentry Projects (Mini Workbook S.)* (Murdoch Books UK, 1998)

Collins Handy DIY (Collins, 2003)

Hylton, Bill, & Matlack, Fred, *Woodworking with the Router* (Guild of Master Craftsmen, 1999)

Jackson, Albert, *Collins Complete DIY Manual* (Collins, 2004)

Jackson, Albert, & Day, David, *Collins Complete Woodworker's Manual* (Collins, 2005)

Joints and Jointmaking: Professional Skills Made Easy (Woodworking Workshops S.) (Hamlyn, 2001)

Lawrence, Mike, *Do It Yourself: Shelves and Storage* (Southwater, 2002)

Mehler, Kelly, *The Table Saw Book* (The Taunton Press, 2003)

Rowley, Keith, *Woodturning: A Foundation Course* (Guild of Master Craftsmen, 1999)

Useful addresses and websites

Health and Safety Executive
www.hse.gov.uk/pubns/
Keep up-to-date with new publications, including free leaflets, from the Health and Safety Commission/Health and Safety Executive – updated weekly.

Woodworking on the Web
www.woodworking.co.uk
The website for woodturners, furniture-makers, woodcarvers and woodworkers everywhere, beginners and experienced alike.

diytools.co.uk
www.diytools.co.uk
Tel: 0151 709 8006
An online site where you can buy anything to do with DIY, including woodworking tools and accessories.

Bob's Woodworking Shop
www.terraclavis.com/bws/
An interesting site for the beginner to browse. Put together by a keen amateur woodworker, the site shows you the set-up he has opted for and raises basic questions often asked by beginners, including giving suggestions for what tools to start with and how to organize your workshop.

Index

Collins need to know?

Further titles in Collins' practical and accessible **Need to Know?** series:

Digital photography
All the kit, techniques and tips you need to take great photographs

192pp   £8.99
PB   0 00 718031 4

Golf
All the kit, techniques and inspiration to get into the game

192pp   £8.99
PB   0 00 718037 3

Zodiac types
Yourself, your friends and your family revealed

192pp   £7.99
PB   0 00 718038 1

Watercolour
All the kit, techniques and inspiration you need to get into painting

192pp   £8.99
PB   0 00 718032 2

Card games
All the rules and tips you need to start playing over 60 card games

192pp   £6.99
PB   0 00 719080 8

Yoga
All the tips and techniques you need to get healthy in mind and body

192pp   £8.99
PB   0 00 719091 3

Pilates
All the tips and techniques you need to get a lithe, flexible body

192pp   £8.99
PB   0 00 719063 8

Guitar
All the gear, techniques and tips you need to play the guitar

192pp   £9.99
PB   0 00 719088 3

DIY
All the know-how you need to get doing it yourself

192pp   £8.99
PB   0 00 719447 1

Weddings
All the facts, advice and inspiration you need for the perfect wedding

208pp   £9.99
PB   0 00 719703 9

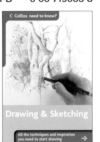

Drawing & Sketching
All the techniques and inspiration you need to start drawing

192pp   £8.99
PB   0 00 719327 0

Birdwatching
All the tips and techniques you need to get into birdwatching

192pp   £8.99
PB   0 00 719527 3

The World
All the maps and facts you need to know in today's world

192pp   £7.99
PB   0 00 719831 0

Dog Training
All the ideas and techniques you need to transform your dog into a well behaved, sociable companion

192pp   £9.99
PB   0 00 719980 5

Knots
All the tips and equipment you need to know how to tie knots

192pp   £9.99
PB   0 00 719979 1

Kama Sutra
All the ideas and techniques you need to enjoy a fantastic sex life

192pp   £9.99
PB   0 00 719582 6

To order any of these titles, please telephone **0870 787 1732**. For further information about all Collins books, visit our website: **www.collins.co.uk**